LITERATURES AND ORATURES AS KNOWLEDGE SYSTEMS

Texts from Northeast India

LITERATURES AND ORATURES AS KNOWLEDGE SYSTEMS

Texts from Northeast India

Edited by
Subha Chakraborty Dasgupta
Goutam Biswas
Samantak Das

AKANSHA PUBLISHING HOUSE
NEW DELHI • GUWAHATI • VISAKHAPATNAM

AKANSHA PUBLISHING HOUSE
4649-B/21, Ansari Road
Daryaganj, New Delhi-110002
Phones: 23268193, 09435116718
Email: ektabooks@yahoo.com
visit us: www.akanshapublishinghouse.com

Literatures and Oratures as Knowledge Systems: Texts from Northeast India

First Published 2011

ISBN 978-81-8370-280-5

PRINTED IN INDIA

Published by Akansha Publishing House, New Delhi-110002 and printed at Harmain Offset Printers, Delhi.

Contents

1. Introduction 1

2. Literatures and Oratures as Knowledge Systems: Texts from the Northeast 4
Mrinal Miri

3. Notes on Tribal World, Truth and Art 12
Sujata Miri

4. Narrative as An/Other History or His/Story Otherwise 20
Sukalpa Bhattacharjee

5. Matrix of Manipuri Culture: Lai-Haraoba of Manipur 32
L. Joychandra Singh

6. Pictorial Representation and Knowledge: Case Study of *Hastividyarnava* 38
Meghali Goswami

7. The Performance of Identity and Histories of Representation 48
Rimli Bhattacharya

8. 'Exotica' or Ethics? Reviewing the Aesthetics and Politics of Contemporary Manipuri Theatre 76
Epsita Halder

9. "The Trickster Figure" in North-Eastern Folklore: Contemporary Transformations in an Ao Naga Short Story 93
Debashree Dattaray

10. A Study of Selected Old Sayings and Narratives of the Mizo: Oral Literature as Knowledge System 114
Margaret Ch. Zama

11. Ethnophilosophy: Conceptual Artefacts, Wisdom and Critique of Anthropocentrism in India's Northeast 121
Prasenjit Biswas

12. Making Sense of the Present through Sanu Lama's *Mṛgatṛṣṇa* 147
Pravesh G. Jung

13. *Ki Jingsneng Tymmen* and the Clan Elder 157
Esther Syiem

14. Generating Knowledge: Khasi-Jaintia Oral Texts 173
Soumen Sen

Our Contributors 190

Index 193

1

Introduction

The Northeast of India is an ethnically-diverse, culturally-rich region that has been less-than-fairly treated in Indian academia (although things seem to be changing somewhat in recent years). Studies of the Northeast have tended to focus on the more exotic, and "foreign", elements of the region, seeing its cultural forms through the lens of anthropological analysis instead of treating the region as a complex, evolving entity whose bewildering range of cultural forms and practices can be examined to gain useful insights into how literary and oral texts allow readers/audiences to enter the region's diverse cultural traditions and pluralistic epistemologies that find expression through literatures and performative traditions.

A literary work of art does not presuppose but encounters a life-world. Presupposition is heuristic, which may sometimes be necessary for philosophical explanation, but literature naturally harbours and therefore is averse to explanation. A philosophy *of* literature may enter into many presuppositions for analytical and explanatory purposes and literary theories tend to be more in proximity with philosophy. The literary world does not inform any philosophy *of* literature but helps us in envisioning a philosophy *in* literature and contributes to philosophy. A work begins in a horizon and crosses it with remnants of the same horizon. It thus contributes to and enriches the cultural memory of a people while pointing to the philosophy *in* it.

The literatures of Northeast India cannot be styled simply as 'romantic' as though projecting the spirit of romantic philosophy like that of, say, Coleridge. If asked, a littérateur of Northeast India will rather speak of the primacy of perception. Within its domain the *world* speaks to the author. But which *world*? This is the world that the author encounters within the bounds of her senses. Through her expressions the bounds expand by deferring the world further and further. She does not *have* an experience *of* language but she experiences *with* language. Highlighting the primacy of perception, Golay's paper in this volume speaks of "philosophy as being qualified by literature" and looks upon literature *as* philosophy.

The nature of this perception permeates the life-world which, in the Northeast's context, has an *untold biography*. It is *untold* because the language-silence negotiation is not rightly explored in the language of common history writing. The littérateurs of Northeast India tell us this biography and contest the mainstream interpretative parameters that do not take cognizance of the meaningful pauses between utterances and sentences in the process of forming a world out of a life-world. They tell us a history in the form of story-telling - a history which is alive and not the type of history written by non-participants in the life-world. The essence of all kinds of aesthetic and discursive exercises of a community in the form of art, history, ethnography, and politics, and is internalized in this story-telling.

One of the purposes of this volume is to bring forth the nature of this story-telling and its types among different ethnic and linguistic communities of Northeast India. The papers collected here study literary and oral texts in terms of a complex of knowledge system that include practical concerns of everyday living along with larger world-views unique to the culture at a specific point of time and suffused with a vision that constantly pushes back the horizons of our mental landscapes. Texts are examined in terms of channels of communication in the development of knowledge and analysed in terms of the material aspects of the text, the patronage it receives, its readership and in general the field of forces within which it operates, along with internal factors such as the configuration of affects and emotions that gives an authentic representative quality to what is being expressed. How the aesthetic percept is shaped into a vision through a particular use of language, and the particular dimensions of the knowledge that is being produced, forms another aspect of the analysis carried out by the contributors to this volume.

Quite obviously, a volume like this cannot claim any kind of comprehensiveness where the literatures and oratures of an area as historically, geographically and culturally diverse as the Northeast is concerned, but it is equally true that such diversity is under threat and it is urgently necessary to preserve and foreground the diverse knowledge systems of the Northeast or such resources may be lost to us forever. It is in the hope of initiating such an exercise, in preserving as well as in analysing, the oratures and literatures of Northeast India that this volume has been prepared.

The papers in this volume emerged out of a seminar held under the Centre of Advanced Study, Department of Comparative Literature, Jadavpur University, in co-operation with Assam University, Silchar and assisted by the Centre for Studies in Social Sciences and the Maulana Abul Kalam Azad Institute of Asian Studies, Kolkata. We gratefully acknowledge the co-operation received from all concerned, particularly from the Vice-Chancellor of Jadavpur University, Professor Pradip Narayan Ghosh, the Vice-Chancellor of Assam University, Professor Tapodhir Bhattacharya, the Director of MAKAIAS, Professor Hari Vasudevan and the Regional Officer-in-Charge of CSSS, Sri Sushanta Ghosh. We are grateful to Dr. Sucheta Bhattacharya Sri Sourabh Chakraborty and Smt. Ratna Chakraborty for their assistance with the manuscript. For errors that remain, we, the editors, are solely responsible.

Editors

2

Literatures and Oratures as Knowledge Systems: Texts from the Northeast

Mrinal Miri

The first point I would like to make is that I am not at all qualified for this job. I am not a literary person. I read literature - primarily fiction and occasionally poetry - but obviously I am not qualified as a literary person. And, as for knowledge systems, perhaps I can say something about it, but not from a position where I am asked to give the keynote address.

I do not know what a keynote address is, what it means. A key is used to open something. I do not know whether what I say will provide you with the key to open anything.

First of all let me say something about modernity as it is something that all of us are concerned with. We are not beyond modernity – even though a few people say that we are now in the age of post-modernity. But I am going to talk about modernity because the idea of the philosophical discipline of epistemology creates the modern. Well, people have talked about knowledge right from the very beginnings of philosophy, whether in the West or in India. But as a discipline within philosophy, epistemology is a modern device. Now, why is it a modern device? Because of the modern conception - let me say something as somebody who is not a modernist but who is fairly a child of modernity.

Modern western culture has often given itself a picture, born in the 18th century Enlightenment, of a civilisation founded on scientific knowledge of the world and rational knowledge which places the highest premium on the individual human life and freedom of thought and belief. And that such freedom and rationality will lead to social progress through self-controlled work creating a better material, political, and intellectual life. I think this is a fairly accurate description of modernity. Accurate, if not absolutely complimentary, which at least is an approving kind of description. This is the point—founded on scientific knowledge of the world and rational knowledge of value. Now, what is this scientific knowledge of the world? Well, I mean, this is the origin of epistemology as a modern act.

Scientific knowledge, as we all know, is a kind of elaborately organised, explicitly theorised thing, what many philosophers might like to call foundational knowledge. What is this foundational knowledge or foundation of knowledge? The question is — how do you know anything at all? How can this knowledge prosper? Such a question can be asked against the background of a particular view of how knowledge can be produced at all.

The simplest view of knowledge is that there is a kind of transaction between the subject and the object. There may be different kinds of transactions between the object and the subject—each transaction is mediated by a procedure. And this procedure produces knowledge of the object. There is the object and here you have the subject and then the two come together. And this is a kind of confrontational view. The object confronts the subject and the subject confronts the object — there is a transaction at this space. This transaction itself is not knowledge — it is a procedure, which is called the rational procedure. Through this process you gain knowledge of the object. Now, this is the foundation of knowledge and scientific knowledge is a theorised, elaborated, thematised elaboration of this foundation.

Now, what is the epistemological problem? The epistemological problem is: how do you know that what this procedure has produced for us is the theory of the object of knowledge? And there are different kinds of knowledge. The procedures must be corrected. And what are the limits of this knowledge? There are people who ask – is this really knowledge? So these are the problems of the discipline of philosophy as far as modernity is concerned. The important thing is the foundation and the confrontation and transaction, which ultimately produce knowledge of the object.

There are lots of people who have questioned this foundation view of knowledge. But I would like to quote from a very unlikely source of the rejection of this modernist view of knowledge. I would like you to guess who that person is.

This is the quote, which is appropriate because this is a lecture. "You come to this lecture room as usual, at the usual hour, and go to your usual place. You hold on to this experience of your 'seeing your place', or else you can likewise put yourself in my place: entering the lecture room I see the lectern... What do I see: brown surfaces intersecting at right angles? No, I see something different—a box, moreover a biggish box, with a smaller box built upon it. No, that's not it at all, I see the lectern at which I am to speak... I see the lectern– I do not see the box upon another box, I do not see a surface... It is not as if I first saw brown intersecting surfaces, which subsequently present themselves to me as a box, then as a speaker's desk, and next as an academic speaker's desk, a lectern, as if, in a manner of speaking, I were sticking the lectern element on the box like a label... I see the lectern at a single stroke, as it were." (Heidegger: 1998: 94-95).

This quote comes from a lecture delivered in 1919 by Martin Heidegger. It is one of his early lectures. Now, I must ask, how can I see the lectern at a single stroke? I can see the lectern at a single stroke because, and this is what Heidegger says, I live in a world of which the lectern is an organic element. A world forms the necessary background of such a scene. A world that has, for instance, educational institutions, that has academic practices of different kinds - libraries, scholarships, seminars and so on. It is only then that I find in the world this lectern. Otherwise if this world was not available to me - this would not be a lectern – this would be another thing. So, it is only because I live in this world where you have educational institutions, colleges, universities and so on, you have academic practices, you have different kinds of libraries, scholarships and so on that I can see the lectern in one stroke. So, it is within such a world, against the background of a non-reflective, non-theoretic knowledge of such a world, that seeing a lectern at one stroke is possible.

From this I sail on to something else, taking this as my cue: to exist, as a human being is to exist in a world. It is the pervasive, non-thematised presence of the world. So, if things are present in this pervasive, non-thematised presence of the world then I see things as meaningful or meaningless, as mattering or non-mattering, as good or bad and find myself obliged to do something or not to do something. It is within such a world that all these things make sense. The primary act of knowledge is not the encounter of the self and the object of knowledge and the abstract procedure completing the act. The possibility of this depends upon my being in the world. The human self is closed in a realm on the one hand, facing an outer realm on the other.

To come to the Northeast tribesman's mind is, as it were, to gain a look into his world. How? How do I get into his world? And this is very interesting because I am a part of the world and it is because I am a part of the world that things make sense to me: things are meaningful; things are meaningless, good bad, right wrong and true false. It might take me a while to explain why true false must also be included; hence I shall not go into it. It is because I am a part of this world that all these things are possible. And now, if I say that the tribesman has his own world and therefore it is within this world that meanings are made - things are meaningful, meaningless, right, wrong, good, bad and so on - how do I gain an entry into this world?

Now, one kind of romantic answer to this question is that I can empathise with the tribesman. It is possible for me to gain an entry into the tribesman's world because it is possible for me to enter his soul – to gain entry into the tribesman's mind, that is empathy as opposed to sympathy. For sympathy you do not have to enter into somebody's mind. You can sympathise with somebody from outside without understanding - without knowing. You can do it. But for an empathetic understanding of somebody it is necessary for you to become that person. Now, how is it possible to become that person? There are two ways in which you can understand empathy. One way is to say that empathy requires that I see things as though I were in his position—that is one way of understanding empathy. Now, how is it possible for me to be in his position? It is for me to be me, not him – that is, I in his position. I am taking my world with me and I am trying to place myself in his position. That is no understanding of him, that is understanding of myself –taking me into his position to understand me. So, that is not empathy. The other way is if I were him – not I as I am now in his position – but if I were to become him. Now for me to be him is to understand a great deal of him before I could imagine myself to be him. I can empathise with my wife because I know a great deal about my wife and if she was a stranger to me I would not be able to empathise. In other words, there must be knowledge before empathy. For empathy I must then already know. Empathy cannot be the only way in which I can know the other person who belongs to another culture, another world.

So, you can think of it as a gradual induction into the world. It requires sympathy certainly and sometimes it is a matter of deliberate effort. For instance, you can think of the great painter Paul Gauguin – for him it was a matter of deliberate effort, not only deliberate effort but a kind of slow, painful deliberate process. And at the end, maybe knowledge and empathy become possible.

You can think of examples here and even in the Northeast. But sometimes there is a natural transition from one world to another. And these natural transitions take place all the time in the Northeast, with the multiplicity of cultures and languages and so on. People have reached into the other world. The process of natural interactions takes place and these produce a fusion of the world. Well, I do not like to use it as phrase, but it produces *understanding* – a sense of commonness, common purposes and so on. I am not a romantic about the past but in our days it is quite clear that such efforts, such interactions did take place. Things can no longer happen as they did, say, even fifty years ago. Now, different forces have come into play. And these are so powerful that nothing, no resources in these cultures, are powerful enough to come to them to resist it, to co-exist.

Now, let me say something about art and language. As we all know, there are many theories about art. I am not going into them. There are many here much better qualified to do this. But let me mention something. What, after all, is Art? Art is representation, art is imitation, mimesis and then, on the other hand, art is a source, a very special kind of spirit and you replace the object and you get the art of the context. Art is also a kind of expression of the subjective feeling of the artist. Art creates subjectivity, intention and so on, I do not know – there are all kinds of criticisms of these views. I am sure there are ways to criticise a book – take the first view – because you are looking for a knowledge system and it is very important to get clear about this view. The view is that art is representation. It represents the world.

Now, think of a work of fiction. Frequently it is said that it is a mirror of the world - it represents the world like a mirror. I mean, think of a great work of fiction as a mirror of the world - think of *Hamlet* as it presents the world. What does this mean? You can reduce *Hamlet* to propositions, true propositions, about the world. *Hamlet* is about angels and about all kind of things and you can go on and on and on listing these propositions out which, ultimately, you would have something that is equivalent to *Hamlet*. Only then *Hamlet* would be mirror of the world, true propositions about the world. Can you think of *Hamlet* in this way? Suppose you have produced a hundred or a million propositions from out of *Hamlet* as true propositions of the world. But has *Hamlet* been exhausted by these propositions? Obviously not, there would be a residue, a necessary residue, which would breed from the essence of *Hamlet*. So, this is one way of showing that art is representation – art as mirror of the world is not really an acceptable view of art. Now, I think of art – it emanates from the world from which/in which/of which art is an inhabitant of the world in my sense – not just in the natural, physical world. Again I use a word from Heidegger: it is an *unconsumed* thing and it is in a sense also a world within the world, a world opening out the world of the tribesman. Therefore literature is all about these things – dances, folk–literature, folk art and so on. You talk about the creativity of all these things. But who is the creator? There is no author – authorship is not the word. The necessary responsibility of the author - what I am saying is not a part of debate. But nonetheless it is important to relate and state whether art is an object of a community, a collectivity – does it make sense at all? Now, think of – I do not know how many people have seen this—think of the Kohrians, a Naga tribe. They are great craftsmen, great sculptors also–their woodcrafts are absolutely fantastic. They are very, very powerful – carvings on boats, carvings on wood and so on. Now, you take this out of the Kohrian world and put it in a museum or in an exhibition—people would say that this is a wonderful work of art. But it is only in the Kohrian world that it is a true sign, I emphasise the term 'true sign'.

Now, think of dance. Most folk-dances have repetitions of the same thing over and over and so on. But think of a folk dance's context and think of its relation to the world, in which the dance is significant, signified. And I think the dance reaffirms the world - the folk-dance reaffirms the life of the community, the importance of the life of the community within a particular culture. And similarly if you think of continuity, within tribal cultures, this continuity is defined in different ways. But one of the ways of a formalist continuity is to say that the past and present and the future are very strongly linked together. The past is not past. That people who are dead are still there–they are there in their world which is absolutely interconnected to our world. They care for us, they watch us and if necessary they punish us and we are responsible for the community because we are also going to that world. So this is what ensures the continuity of the world – there are no separate things in this world. For us, moderns, death is a separate thing–my death means the death of the world. But for the tribesman, death is a passage into life, which is entered into this world. So think of different kinds of rituals, if you like, storytelling, events and so on. These can be looked at in this possible way and I think our understanding of these cultures can benefit us.

Now I wish to say a little bit at the end about language. Language is a thing in terms of which I really enact the world of the community. There is no other way – it must be through language. We can become absolutely, totally clear. This clarity is something that I would like to say about the tribal world. Tribal culture is depicted in its language. The language in any speech– the entire language is present. The whole language, as it were, reincorporates what I say and thus is significant. So the openness of meaning is very important which is also delicate. When you are trying to understand a poem—there are degrees of depth of understanding. There are many significant connections you make. The world of the poem needs uncovering and this is the process.

Think of a name index—it is possible for a computer. But is it possible for it to make a thematic index of a poem or a thematic index of a great literary work? Obviously, it is not possible for it to make a thematic index of a folk-narrative or of a folk-song. Because the world has numerous connections of languages, language has an organic existence in such a way that whatever you have is the entire language itself.

I come to my last point. The tribesman cannot be forced into his world. It comes from his hidden practices, his songs and his stories and so on unlike the so-called "universal" scientific knowledge. It is necessary for us to understand this aspect of tribal culture.

So, language is complete by its completeness —what is meant by that is whatever I say in this language can be said in utter clarity. There are so many things you can say in French, which cannot be said in Bengali. Many other things can be said in Bengali, which I cannot say in my language. So you have to learn another language and then turn it into your language and I think this is what is called the fusion of horizon.

This is the world and you cannot say there is only darkness, there is only chaos. That will be a blind reaction. No thinking, or no knowledge will be possible then. Then what would be left? Only civilisations, which are 200 or 300 years old, will be recognised but not other communities and cultures.

REFERENCE

Heidegger, Martin, *Collected Works,* trans. Safranksi, 1998.

3

Notes on Tribal World, Truth and Art

Sujata Miri

While in the case of the more complex or the so-called civilized societies, there is available for the social scientist to study, their traditional sacred texts along with their hermeneutical interpretations, the same is not true for most of the so-called primitive societies. The absence of a written intellectual tradition should not lead us to the conclusion that they lacked a complex system of rules of behaviour, of rights and duties. Their worldview represents a framework or a conceptual system which offers answers to questions such as: who am I? Who are others? What is my relationship to others? It contains guidelines about man-god, man-woman, man-child, man-nature relationships. Contrary to the popular belief a tribal worldview has a coherence and completeness which can be ascertained by gaining access to the inner life of the people.

All aspects of the life of the tribal in the traditional system, constituted by language and custom, were covered in the wide framework of his religion. In one sense it can be said that religion was the centre of his cultural life. Most interesting to note is the fact that one can discover in traditional tribal religions strong sanctions for the preservation of their ecology. This is connected with their unquestioned respect for nature, man and animal. The Khasis, for example seems in their world-view to commit themselves to a belief in the existence of an all- pervasive order and a law operating in this world. There are intelligible connections between different courses and orders of events in the world. Human societies also conform to this all-pervasive order and human activities are regulated in terms of rules, which are the expressions of the general order. Neither man nor God can deflect the course of law through their power. The preservation of the order or "system" of nature thus acquires a sacred aspect and this aspect is embodied in elaborate rules relating to man's interaction with nature.

Modern rationality demands unificatory epistemologies and homogenization of evidence which it hopes will one day lead automatically to the unification of the world. Undoubtedly universalism of any kind attempts to dispel the threat of cognitive anarchy but there are underlying problems associated with it. No matter how attractive this conception is, it just so happens that there is such a variety of cultural systems in the world that anthropologists and others despaired of ever finding any universal traits. They found the cognitive equipment of other cultures, especially, folk, tribal or indigenous cultures, as at best incomplete, if not totally erroneous. With the arrival of relativism we have started taking cultures other than our own more seriously. Prior to this academic journey, we have the tribal identified as an animist simply because he 'sees spirits everywhere' believes in ghosts and generally lives in a world of fear and suspicion.

The source of this misunderstanding is the failure to identify the vision of life that tribal culture represents. I call it the traditional vision, which sees God man and nature as inextricably linked. This vision declares, "It is the same I which reverberates in all" and that all living creatures are animated by a common indwelling spirit. This vision I wish to emphasize, can form the basis of an authentic spiritual and moral experience. The tribal religions are concerned more with the well-being of a well-knit world comprising man, animal and nature than with personal salvation. This would be incomprehensible to someone who is schooled in modernity which places man at the center of the universe isolated both from God and nature.

The first point of agreement in different tribal worldviews is the emphasis on the sameness (qualitative) of man, god and nature. Indeed the myths of creation speak of the love between the pairs of Sky-God and Earth-Goddess (*Sitking-Kedding and Peddo-*

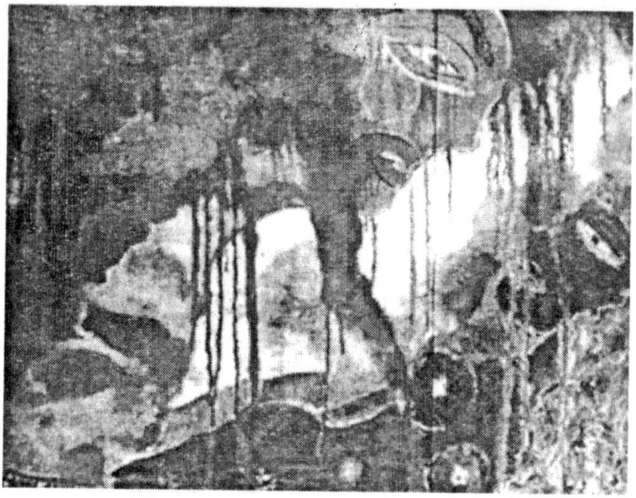

Dodum), the Sun-Goddess and the Earth-God, their voluntary separation from each other so that there be room for others to grow and flourish.

Other legends describe mountains, rivers and clouds as beings that felt, perceived and deliberated as persons. The *Akas* of Arunachal Pradesh for example identify the sky, mountains, earth and rivers as the highest gods. I will use as illustration two stories from the rich depository of Khasi legends in the following pages which give us important insights into their world-view: There lived the two most handsome mountain gods named *U Syiemper Nongsyih* and *U Symper Kmawan*, facing each other with a smile, reputed to be the greatest of friends.

When U Kmawan wanted to get married, a match was arranged between him and the beautiful *Ka Iewma*. They lived happily together doing their duties of protecting their neighbours from evil forces.

On getting the news that his father was seriously ill, *U Kmawan* had to visit his ailing father. While leaving, he cautioned his wife to behave in a discretionary manner. In his absence his friend, *U Nongsynrih*, finding her alone and as beautiful as the moon, fell in love with her. On his return, the husband found the lovers: the wife and his friend. The fight between the two gods began.

They started to shoot at each other with bows and arrows. For nine days and nine nights this continued without a break.

At last *U Kmwan* was victorious over *U Nongsynrih*. Victory was his because his cause was just while *U Nongsynrih* was in the wrong. Accordingly having been kicked in the hip by *U Kmwan* he lies at the foot of the hill even to this day.

There is another story about the competition between two river goddesses: they challenged each other as to who will reach the plains of Sylhet first.

The younger sister called *Umiam* was proud. She felt that she was strong and powerful enough to cut a channel for herself straight through the rocky hills, which blocked the way.

Feeling overconfident and incautious she plunged deeper and deeper into the mountainous terrain.

Though wasting her time while digging her course, her confidence did not leave her till she looked up and saw her elder sister dancing away in joy, glistening like a silver necklace.

As the elders tell the story they emphasize the two underlying motives of the story, which are the welfare of mankind and to caution rash and ignorant individuals against hasty and indiscretious acts, by showing the victory of the more diligent and steady older sister.

My paintings may not provide a crucial point of access to fundamental truths about the world and what it is to be human. They may be seen as a naïve attempt at appropriation of tribal tradition, as a sort of retelling. While looking at them, however, we must stand guard against hastily pressing them into our own expectations of meaning, only then can we allow the tradition's own meaning to be heard.

There is a strong tradition in history of philosophy, which puts art and truth at opposing ends of a spectrum. Art is downgraded to the status of an amusement and an entertainment, in no way contributing to a profound understanding of the world. Plato puts in the mouth of Socrates the view that art deceitfully sells itself as truth but is in fact dangerously distorting. For him philosophical wisdom is the only way to truth; philosophers by virtue of their direct and undistorted knowledge through apprehension of the Forms, have an unmediated grasp of the varying degrees of reality. This has led to a tradition of philosophers who are suspicious of all forms of art, especially when they parade as accesses to the realm of the real. In *The Critique of Judgment*, Kant works on the assumption that art is fundamentally concerned with feeling. Personally I would rather take my inspiration from philosophers such as Heidegger and his idea of art as a primordial engagement with truth. Art discloses, like truth itself, an opening up to the world, it uncovers truth about ourselves that no amount of scientific endeavor can reveal.

4

Narrative as An/Other History or His/Story Otherwise

Sukalpa Bhattacharjee

Urvashi Butalia in tracing the silenced voices of partition victims looks for a methodology for retrieving their voice and finds it in James E. Young's account of the Holocaust.[1] She says that one could know this event called Partition from the ways 'it has been handed down to us'. It is through fiction, memoirs, testimonies, individual and collective memories that one could weave together the fragments of the moment called Partition which has only been the beginning of many other partitions – of land, of history, of people, of hearts and of selves. Like many other geo-political and cultural locales affected by Partition, a very unique site for such an inquiry is the geo-political locale called the Surma-Barak Valley which has witnessed the added burden of the Sylhet Referendum as a legitimized corollary of Partition. In the wake of the Partition Assam happily gave away one of its districts Sylhet to Pakistan. Mountbatten's partition-plan announced on 3 June 1947, provided inter-alia for a referendum to be held in the Sylhet district of Assam to decide whether it should remain a part of the Indian province of Assam or go to East Pakistan. The farcical Sylhet referendum was held on 6 July 1947 and the predictable result went in favour of a merger with Pakistan. While the umbilical chord of the vast chunk of the Hindu and Muslim population belonging to the four *thanas* that were retained from the Sylhet District by Assam remained connected to Sylhet, politically and geographically they remained attached to the Cachar District of Assam i.e. Barak Valley. Therefore, Surma-Barak Valley becomes an appropriate description for a cultural intervention through literary narrative and fictional descriptions of the moment of Partition. Such an enterprise not only deconstructs a dominant historical moment but also recasts it, weaving different levels of silences.

Literary representations have always highlighted the difference between the *real* and *imaginary* that lies at the heart of the self by way of covering it up through a complex play between the symbolic and the experiential. The play has a double bind: *of* setting-to-work in memory and *of* temporally implicated arrival of an event. The play emerges as an experience preserving system of signification which can take a linguistic, semiotic and literary stance on the very notion of Being. This is how literary narratives essentially link real life form to art. Such narratives, if domain specific and therefore coherent, are likely to constitute a community that identifies itself with the narrative in terms of a remembered tradition, an event or a collective memory. Narratives derive their sustenance not because they essentially speak of something that is true or false but because they make their listeners feel a sense of shared meaning. Rather than being a simple case of the storyteller and the narrative in question, inventing and imposing metaphors of agreement, what perhaps actually guide and determine the character of the narrative to be told are the traces of lived experiences with all their knowable and unknowable elements. Ingrained within the narratives, the issue, one presumes, calls for a dialogue between a thinking self and a fixed notion of authentic community. Such dialogues are expected to bring to the fore all the implicit and explicit elements that account for the space between the narrative, its teller and the target audience. Such exercises basically centre on/in tracing the moments of presence and absence of the self, the world and others in an interlocution between the text and the context. It may eventually lead one to possibly end up finding a number of breaks and interruptions within what has so far looked like a coherent story. Consequently, the stable transmission of a fixed essence gives way to a live crisscrossing of signifiers over a dynamic and wide variety of narratives.

Narratives, by virtue of an excess over the comprehension of the tradition, often contain an element of ex-centricity, which implies that they are simultaneously culturally rooted and yet produce a counter-cultural domain. While it allows one to speak and not just say what one means, it promotes listening to the unheard, interprets the truth of the world and self in a way that is often unique. In a constant shift between being and becoming without a realized essence, a realm of the counterfactual therefore automatically goes into it signifying a series of contingent, invented and non-narratable ensemble of experiences. Narratives thus, provide for the necessary double bind of belonging to a unified story of life and yet not belonging to what the story merely says. It opens up a different space of living that looks for different cultures, communities other than one's own and engages one with stories/ narratives of others. This is how narratives emerge as alter/native spaces of enquiry, privileging the representations of everyday life, thereby interrogating the authorial voice of History of an event like Partition. In tracing an alter/native space against dominant texts of history what is needed is a thoroughly discursively informed reading and writing practice that is attentive to the literariness of narrative and the undecidability of all texts.

In this context an examination of a short fiction called *Bindu Bindu Jal*[2] (which means drops of water) by Shekhar Das would provide for an alter/native reading of India's Partition, as experienced by the people under the conditions described above, who were forcibly pushed into refugee-hood causing violation to their material and moral self. The goal of this reading, therefore, is to provide an example of how a staged dialogue between literary and historiographical narratives puts pressure on totalizing constructions of the self, experience, and agency and their relation to the notion of citizenship in the modern nation-state. This is a painful narrative of how a community of people was violently (re)constituted as a monolithic site for the containment of contradictions in state and community nationalist imaginings. Recently, efforts to 'recover' marginal 'voices' and/or memories of the Partition have emphasized the value of including literary sources as 'evidence' in historiographical narratives. More often than not, however, the inclusion of these sources has been engineered to reinscribe humanist notions of literary production as merely subjective, mimetic and universal in contrast to the objectivity and specificity associated with historical research. A narrative like *Bindu Bindu Jal* presents a graphic picture of a community in its moment of ontological loss which results into a total fragmentation of the being. Such a description represents people's individual lives as something separate from their cause, i.e. Partition. Dominant narratives of History have only recorded factual details of Partition leaving out the element of human agony leading to a loss and partition of the self. 'Personal experience,' in this context, is conceived of as universal, transparent and outside language, culture, and ironically, history.[3] Stories of victims take the existence of individuals as real actors whose empirical experiences constitute the history of a people, prompting a 'willing suspension of disbelief.'[4] So rather than asking how conceptions of selves (of subjects and identities) are produced one becomes a participant in the narrative which operates within an ideological construction that not only makes individuals the starting point of knowledge, but that also naturalizes categories such as *man* and *woman*, irrespective of their caste and religion, by treating them as given characteristics of individuals.

The text opens with a familiar symbol of a oil lamp under a basil plant where Surabala is pouring more oil than is necessary so that the lamp can remain lit for the next two days unless disturbed by the wind. The tension of Partition has been introduced by the impending instability of the oil lamp which is a marker of the instability that is to come in the life of the people of the household in particular and the community in general. Surabala and her three children are leaving their home – their ancestor's land – to escape from communal riots and killing. Surabala's husband had already left home to look for shelter and accommodation in the new land. As twelve-year-old Parul, Surabala's youngest daughter, already very angry that her father has left without telling her, watches her mother leave her huge bunch of keys under the basil plant praying to God to look after their home in their absence she wonders why her mother was doing so. Perhaps she was even more perplexed when her mother picked up the keys again saying to herself, 'Let me take back the keys. Maybe it will be possible to come back home again.' Unable to resist her curiosity Parul asks her mother, 'Where are we going maa?' Her mother says, 'India.'

Parul replies, confused, 'But maa, isn't this also India?' 'Yes,' says her mother. 'Everything is the same. Only the name has changed.' The ambivalence of belonging and un-belonging is the state of existence for the victims of Partition where the self becomes a product of the politics of naming. Self becomes the other in the politics of naming, citizens become refugees, one's own land becomes a foreign land just as the symbol of the oil lamp gets disfigured and extenuated into an image of the funeral pyre meant for Parul.

Shekhar Das gives a very poignant description of the journey of Surabala and her three children from home to an unknown and uncertain locale across the border in a bullock cart. Little Parul drops little rags, spoons and pieces of her bangles as the cart moves towards the border explaining that she would use them as landmarks to get back home whenever there was a chance. Little did she imagine that in a few hours she would be cremated in the most unceremonious manner on a river bank after being attacked by cholera. Her mother and brothers could not even provide her with a drop of drinking water amidst the unhygienic environment of the refugee camp. Little Parul, so full of life a little while ago, lies lifeless on the twigs to be lighted as her funeral pyre. As her mother Surabala bathes her for the last time on the river bank, dressing her in her white frock, this lifeless body of a twelve year old child becomes the blank page on which the violent history of Partition will be inscribed. The dominant narrative of history would have no space for this heartbreaking episode of the brutal exodus of people who have lost everything in the real sense of the term. Shekhar Das plays on this image of loss and nothingness through his title, *Bindu Bindu Jal* or drops of water, which represents the drops of silent tears shed by Surabala and many other victims as their little ones die in front of their eyes without even a drop of drinking water. The image of the still flame of the oil lamp under the basil plant at the beginning of the narrative extends to the funeral pyre of many Paruls while invisible flames of grief start blazing in many a mother's heart. The tension between text and context that impinges on fictional accounts of Partition demands that the reader theorize representations of experience taking into account the gap or shift between the text and its historical referent.[5] These sufferings of displaced peoples can be understood as examples of material reality putting pressure on the discursive domains of conservative-nationalism, communalism, and patriarchy. The death of minor children like Parul in refugee camps and the impossibility of postal communication, as in the case of Parul's brother writing a letter to his father Nalini in an imaginary address, to convey the tragedy of his sister's death, present new social and moral issues concerning civic rights in the aftermath of Independence which had its implications in the nationalist imaginings of the recently-formed postcolonial state. In short, the 'everyday' perspective or experience represented in literary narrativizations of these events should be read as a diffraction of historical moments where nations, communities, families, and individuals engage in a discursive struggle over the interpretation of material reality and the identities of 'nowhere people'.[6]

Running parallel with the narrative of Surabala's family are other narratives of people of a small village consisting of twenty houses. The people of this village could not cast their votes on the day of the referendum. On the one hand it was raining heavily on the day of voting and on the other hand it was all managed by false voters. The tension started after midnight when grandchildren had already fallen asleep after story-telling sessions of their grandmothers, farmers had just fallen into slumber least expecting the horror that was waiting although one knew that things were not going right in those days of referendum. The majority of the people of this village are basically peaceful in nature and if there was an attack from the majority group of violators, they could only play defensively. So when the sounds of commotion drew near, the villagers all old and young ran for life seeking shelter and cover behind the bamboo bushes which the jackals had just deserted as if in fear of the violent drama of bloodbath caused by human beings. The most vulnerable were the old who could not run fast and those women with young children in their laps. Violence was unleashed all around. The attackers came with pointed spears and daggers beheading husbands in front of their wives and mutilating the genital organs of both males and females.

The most tragic of all is the story of Basumati and her

husband Dwijen who realize that in their desperate run for life Basumati had picked up her three year old son Ratul's side pillow instead of the sleeping child. As they look to run back to the village to pick him up they see the whole village ablaze. Basumati turns completely insane after days of waiting for her husband to return with her son. Even birds seem to shudder at the condition of Basumati, now completely out of her mind and without any sensation of pain or shame which categorize one as being human. She sleeps under trees and runs around throwing stones unable to even remember her name when officials in the relief camp ask her. Shekhar Das in his narrative of brutal violence and its inscription on the human body, particularly the female (as shown in the case of little Parul and now Basumati), constantly harps on the borderline of the human and the animal. As human beings are reduced to animalism in their mad instinct for violence animals are depicted as possessing the so-called human values. Like the jackals who had run away from the bamboo bushes on seeing the mad killing of man by man, now birds seem to spread their wings and cover the almost naked body of Basumati who even in her insanity cannot escape sexual violence on her body. The irony of the situation is heightened by the fact that another child orphaned by the violence has got attached to Basumati who is not in a state even to be conscious of her own self. Yet she is the proxy mother to this boy who might have lost his own mother in the exodus just as Basumati has lost her son Ratul and whose name she still remembers.

Madness as destruction of human sanity has been understood by many as an inseparable aspect of a collective madness accompanying the violence during and after Partition.[7] Sadaat Hasan Manto in his short story *Khuda Ki Kasam* (I Swear by God) written in the backdrop of Partition depicts a mad mother wandering from city to city in North India, mumbling incoherently, half naked and hair matted just like Basumati refusing to believe that her child is dead. This is how the Partition has resulted in a 'partition of selves' by partitioning families and communities.[8] Under such as partitioning of the self and the border crossing of human and animal values one wonders as to what would be the epistemic status of Reason or rationality of what was 'right' and what was 'wrong', what 'moral' and 'immoral', what 'sane' and what 'insane'. Partition narratives of this kind perhaps destabilize the conventional claim to the ontology of the self and knowledge claims.

Ones claim to narrative as an/other history stems from such destabilization of dominant knowledge systems such as History and the grand narratives of epistemology in its attempt to grasp and represent the element of pain and human suffering that are involved in Partition and Holocaust. Narratives of the fictional kind such as *Bindu Bindu Jal* capture these moments of human pain and suffering without laying truth claims like History.[9] In this context it may be pertinent to recall De Man's argument on literary narratives,[10] that '[w]henever this autonomous potential of language can be revealed by analysis, we are dealing with literariness and, in fact with literature as the place where this negative knowledge about the reliability of linguistic utterance is made available.' Again 'Literature,' de Man writes, 'is fiction not because it somehow refuses to acknowledge 'reality', but because it is not *a priori* certain that language functions according to principles which are those, or which are like those, of the phenomenal world.... This does not mean that fictional narratives are not part of the world and of reality; their impact upon the world may well be all too strong for comfort. What we call ideology is precisely the confusion of linguistic with natural reality, of reference with phenomenalism.' For more than a decade now critical study is being encouraged in claiming an/other history through narrative by critiquing the 'assumed differences between 'literary' versus 'historical' narratives and the assumed 'value' that each 'type' of text comes to represent for the historiographer reconstructing the events of a particular historical moment.'[11] Such a critique of the subjectivity associated with a literary narrative and the objectivity associated with History pronounces the subjects at the receiving end of such an enterprise. These subjects are the victims, the real authors as witness to such an event as Partition and ones claim to an/other history is to give history back to its real authors to whom it actually belongs but who have been turned into the *other* of dominant History.

In such a context the figure of 'Basumati' as the real witness of the violent history of Partition, now turned as its other because of her insanity represents the 'unrepresentable' both in the sense of an impossibility of 'being' as well as of a distorted and victimized *affect* of not having the 'being'. 'Having' assumes a settled history and an autonomous determination of oneself, which remains 'suspended' as an affect of a history of violence. The 'violated' being of Basumati acts as a signifier of victimhood. The question is, can the violated signifier signify its usual historical, objective and cultural reference, or does it just enact the impossibility of representation of its originary suffering of violence? Shekhar Das almost but not completely ventures into a zone of impossibility between signifying and suspension without a passage from reality to history. He poses the signifier 'Basumati' as the sign of being the violated 'mother earth'. The artistic alteration between Basumati as a violated personhood and Basumati as the mother earth is the phenomenology of silence that seeks a new addressee, the institution of nation-state that must listen through Basumati's deaf-mute silence. The situation of Basumati in Sekhar Das's *exposé* can be read along Lyotard,

> (...) [S]omething "asks" to be put into phrases [Basumati], and suffers from the wrong of not being able to be put into phrases right away. This is when the human beings who thought they could use language as an instrument of communication learn through the feeling of pain which accompanies silence (...) that they are summoned by language (...) to recognize that what remains to be phrased exceeds what they can precisely phrase, and that they must be allowed to institute idioms which do not yet exist.[12]

Basumati as an idiom of partitioned selves, assumes the role of singular-plural that institutes a new addresse of nation-state to which it seeks to belong by annulling the partition that it had suffered from. The 'truth' disclosed in this annulment is a 'structure of feeling' that stands as 'evidence' for the 'agency' of the violated.[13] Such an 'evidence' stands over and against the field of a universalizable norm of 'legitimacy' in the conceptual dichotomy of being a person and being an 'other' within the differentiated nation-space constituted by a 'civil society' as an end-in-itself.[14] As argued by philosophers, a rationally coherent 'civil society' as an end-in-itself does not necessarily give a 'face' to its own dialectic, it rather remains as an absence in terms of a relationship within the 'civic' modern society.[15] The most significant ontological-historical question that such a new addresse in the form of a nation-state has to face is, can there be a 'guiltless' relationship with the Other? Or rather, how the guilt would hang before and after every relationship with the Other is the proper substance of a history of violence that looks for 'moral elbow room' in the legislation of the 'self' that is independent of any objectively real feature of the 'violated'.[16] Shekar Das looks for this 'moral elbow room' by altering the violated Basumati into *Basumati* proper with a causal-historical narrative only to be subsumed under an autonomy of self-legislation by partitioned selves. There is, then, a moment of recovery from the impossible 'object' of violence and violation that marks a transition from Basumati, the violated, into Basumati, the mother earth, only to alter and subject the latter in the autonomy of the former (which is independent of the 'object' of violence and history). The situation is better stated in separating the experiential and the 'formation of subjectivity' in a space of the recoverable, the extended notion of the possibility of relationship with a new addressee *that happens only in a new metonymic space*, which is not a space of nostalgia and fantasy – rather it is a space of multiple subjectivities that compose it by a play between the real and the imagined. The meaning of this space can be understood in the following,

> (...) all differential identity will be constitutively split; it will be the crossing point of the logic of difference and the logic of equivalence.[17]

The constitutive split in *Basumati* between speaking and silence, between past and present is an 'unrepresentable' that poses the Lyotardian differend between Basumati's self and Basumati proper that keep crossing each other in the play between the logic of identity and the logic of difference as a co-occurring history in the metonymic space of the face, body, civil society and the nation-state.

NOTES & REFERENCES

1. Urvashi Butalia: *The Other Side of Silence: Voices from the Partition of India.* 2000, p .7.

2. Shekhar Das, *Bindu Bindu Jal,* Amritlok Sahitya Parishad, Kolkata. 2004. As a reader one finds traces and identifies the source of this narrative in the experiences of people of the Surma-Barak Valley who were victimized and displaced due to the (manipulated) verdict of the Sylhet Referendum. However this narrative is not to be read exclusively as the experiences of the people of the Surma-Barak Valley.
3. See Ian Talbot, "Literature and the Human Drama of the 1947 Partition", *South Asia* 18 (1995): 37-56.
4. This is a concept borrowed from S.T. Coleridge meaning a compulsion of a narrative moment that forces the listener to believe in the narrative truth.
5. See Joan W. Scott's "The Evidence of Experience." *Critical Inquiry* 17 (1991).
6. This term is being used as a metaphor by contemporary critics to designate displaced people particularly those rendered homeless after Partition.
7. See Stephen Alter, "Madness and Partition: The Short Stories of Sadaat Hasan Manto", *Alif: Journal of Comparative Poetics*, No. 14, Madness and Civilization, (1994), pp. 91-100.
8. See Vinay Lal, "Partitioned Selves, Partitioned Pasts: A Commentary on Ashis Nandy's Death of an Empire" in Vinay Lal (ed.) *Dissenting Knowledges, Open Futures: The Multiple Selves and Strange Destinations of Ashis Nandy*, Delhi: Oxford, 2000.
9. See Paul Ricoeur's *Time and Narrative,* Vol 3. Trans. Kathleen Blamey and David Pellauer. Chicago, University of Chicago Press. 1988.
10. See Paul de Man's *The Resistanc.. to Theory*, Minneapolis: U of Minnesota 1986, as quoted by Jill Didur in "Fragments of Imagination: Re-thinking the Literary in Historiography through Narratives of India's Partition." in *Jouvert*: Vol. I, Issue 2. 1997.
11. *Ibid.*
12 Jean Francois Lyotard, *The Differend: Phrases in Dispute*, trans. Georges Van Den Abbeele, Univ. of Minnesota Press, Minneapolis, 1980, p. 13.
13. Gayatri Chakravorty Spivak, "Moving Devi-1997: The Non-Resident and the Expatriate," *Other Asias*, Basil Blackwell, Oxford, 2008, p.191.

14. Goutam Biswas, "Autonomy of Reason and Ethics of the Face: Imagining a Civil Society in Kantian Lineage" in Bindu Puri and Heiko Sievers (eds.), *Reason, Morality and Beauty: Essays on the Philosophy of Immanuel Kant*, Oxford University Press, New Delhi, 2007, pp. 34-5

15. Goutam Biswas formulates this following Levinas. *Ibid.*, p. 36-7.

16. Bijoy H. Boruah, "Autonomy and the Virtue of Self-Legislation" in Bindu Puri, *op.cit.*, pp.118-33.

17. Ernest Laclau, *Emancipations*, Verso, London, 1996, p.53.

5

Matrix of Manipuri Culture: Lai-Haraoba of Manipur

L. Joychandra Singh

The *Lai-Haraoba* festival of Manipur deserves to be placed as the most traditional, basic and important festival of the Meiteis, the valley people of Manipur. For a number of reasons, it represents the heart and mind of Meitei philosophy and culture. The ancient Manipuri concept of God as narrated in the Lai-Haraoba tradition reflects a great awareness of divinity. The supreme creator whom the Meiteis called Atiya Guru Sidaba (Guru, the Immortal Sky) is considered by the Meiteis as having both the masculine and feminine qualities. Thus was sung of Him by the Meiteis:

With His hair tied in front
He is the Father
When tied at the back
He is the Mother
When at the crown of the head
He is the Guru.

Meiteis are god-fearing people. In the early days they worshipped their ancestors who were considered as gods or incarnations of gods. Each of the clans had its own place of worship where the image of its deity is installed. Lai-Haraoba has its origin in the tradition of ancestor worship followed by the Meiteis. Lai-Haraoba is performed for the *Lais* (Gods). The four Meitei guardianship lais are collectively called maikei ngakpa (guardians of the directions). The maikei ngakpa are mentioned frequently in the lyrics of Lai-Haraoba. Koubru is the guardian of the north-west. Thangjing is the god of the South-West. Wangbren is the god of the South-East. Marjing is the guardian of the North-East. In addition, Loiyarakpa and Chingkhei-ningthou are also considered as principal deities of the directions. Whenever people offer any worship these deities are remembered. Over and above these deities there are several other local Lais worshipped by several groups of families. These are known as Umang Lais (Sylvan gods), because the places of worship of these gods are in reserved areas, near or inside the localities, surrounded usually by a rich grove of trees which look like a tiny forest.

During the annual festivities of Lai-Haraoba people of the locality gather at the Umang (forest) for the celebration. The history of some of the local deities tell us that they were men with divine attainments. By worshipping their spirit after death, people derive satisfaction of worshipping God through His human representatives. Every deity has his or her background. At the time of annual festivities, the priests sing of the deities and legendary glories. In fact, Lai-Haraoba is a ritual performance which aims at pleasing the gods and goddesses and in turn, it leads to the process of merry-making or rejoicing on the part of the gods and goddesses (*Lai* means gods and goddesses, H*araoba* means rejoicing or pleasing).

Lai-Haraoba festival starts in the Manipuri month of Kalen (April-May) and may continue to June. Each festival normally lasts from 3-5 days to even one month. The area where a Lai-Haraoba performance takes place is called Laipham. There are about 364 laiphams in Manipur (some place it at about 400). They are found scattered all over the valley. In every laipham there is a laishang (shrine). In the shrine there are two presiding deities, Lainingthou and Lairembi. The two images are covered with brass masks. The whole ritual is organised in front of these deities. Nine laibungthous (gods), seven lainuras (goddesses), other guardian deities are supposed to be present in the Lai-Haraoba while the supreme God, Atiya Guru Sidaba, would grace the performance with His presence. Generally, there are four forms of Lai-Haraoba: Kanglei Haraoba (performed in major parts of the valley of Manipur), Moirang Haraoba (performed only in Moirang about 45 kilometers from Imphal), Kakching Haraoba (observed in Kakching about 40 Kilometers from Imphal), and Chakpa Haraoba (performed at the scheduled caste areas). As regards the ritual observances, there are differences in all the four types of Lai-Haraoba. However, the basic structure is the same. Differences are only on local variations.

In a way Lai Haraoba may be regarded as a fertility rite. Through this, the Meiteis seek the favour of Gods and Goddesses for procreativity. They believe that its observance would lead to fertility in the life of man himself. They also believe that it would lead to a good harvest and would bring a healthy communal life. Accordingly, rain imageries figure quite prominently in the songs of Lai-Haraoba. Moreover, male and female symbolism, depicting procreation, also pervades its rituals and lyrics.

It is also significant that Lai Haraoba takes place during spring at the onset of the rains. Meiteis used to believe that the sky is the male component while earth the female one – both being symbolized as the father and the mother principles – from whose passionate union come forth the vegetation and all the crops which sustain humanity. Such fertility rites would naturally be resorted to with a view to increasing the fertility of the soil for a bountiful harvest, bringing timely rains and mitigating natural calamities. Basically, Lai Haraoba would stress on this fertility aspect of the ritual from start till finish.

The sequences of Lai-Haraoba may be described as follows: First, prior permission of the Pandit Loisang (the Palace Department of Pandits) is necessary before the start of the festival; second, dressing of the deities (Lai Phi shetpa) would be done; third, calling up of the spirit from water, either a pond or river, would be completed (Lai Eekouba). After this, the Festival will begin and the daily rituals include the following: First, the deity is awakened with the singing of pena music (Yakeiba); in the afternoon dances are presented (Laibou Jagoi, Lairel Mathek Jagoi, Phibul Ahabi etc.). The sequences then continue. A ritual part called Kanglei Thokpa and Lam Thokpa (literally 'deity does outing') take place. This is done either on the fifth, seventh, ninth or eleventh day of Lai Haraoba according to the number of days the Festival is performed. The final day is called Lairoi. On this day all the daily rites would be repeated. The festival continues well past midnight and by almost day break the last rite Nongarol (return of the deity back to heaven) takes places. All the audience will assemble around the shrine as the Maibi (priest) sings, beseeching the deities to return to their heavenly abode. After the return of the Lais (gods) to their celestial abode Saroi Khangba (appeasement of the spirits) is performed and thus the Festival comes to an end.

There are several books on Lai-Haraoba published in Manipuri describing the ritual forms and sequences, the lyrics used in the performance, and of course the role of Maiba, Maibi and Penakhongba. Lai-Haraoba is conducted by three functionaries: Maiba (Priest), Maibi (Priestess) and Penakhongba (the player of the traditional musical instrument called Pena). The female maibi plays a more important role in the festival than her male counterpart. A woman can become a maibi either by choice or by being possessed by the lai (God). Maibis require intensive training under able Gurus. They are believed to be able to communicate the messages of gods and goddesses during the trances. Such 'communications' are done before a mass gathering like the Lai-Haraoba. The other mode of communication is like the practice of fortune-telling. In the society a maibi is addressed respectfully as ima (mother). All the rituals in Lai-Haraoba are conducted by maibis. Male maibis (nupa maibis) are also recognised by the society. Thus maibi is essentially a medium, a link between the natural and supernatural and cannot be judged by sex. Nupa maibis are to dress themselves like women. All members of this cult are known only as maibis, whether they are men or women. The role of Penakhongba (player of pena music) is also distinctive in Lai-Haraoba. His presence at Lai-Haraoba is as important as that of maibi and maiba. In Lai-Haraoba, Penakhongba plays to accompany some of the dances, chanting the sacred lyrics to his own playing. Indeed, he provides musical accompaniment to the ritual sequences throughout the duration of Lai-Haraoba.

I would like to mention two books published in English during the last decade on Lai-Haraoba of Manipur. The first book was published in 1997 by Vikas Publishing House, New Delhi under the title *The Pleasing of the Gods* authored by Saroj N. Arambam Parratt and John Parratt. The second book, published in Imphal in 2001, under the caption *Lai-Haraoba of Manipur* was authored by Ratan Kumar. The two books give a detailed account of Lai-Haraoba, its anatomy and sequences, the lyrics and songs, the ritual practices, the inner philosophy and the importance of Lai-Haraoba, its structural pattern and modes of organisation, piece by piece, step by step. The two texts would give a vital clue to anyone who wishes to venture into the matrix of Manipuri culture and civilization as enshrined in the performance of Lai-Haraoba. Books on Manipuri culture written in English are rare and in this regard the two texts would fill up the dearth to a great extent.

Another text was brought out in 2005 by Nongthombam Premchand published by Cultural Resource Centre, Imphal. The name of the book is *Rituals and Performances (Studies in Traditional Theatres of Manipur*. Here the author gives a new interpretation and systematic analysis of the popular Manipuri festival Lai-Haraoba and emphatically proves that Lai-Haraoba is the best form of traditional Manipuri theatre. He says that Lai-Haraoba is a ritual theatre of Manipur: it is a ritual performance and also a theatre. The author says that the various elements like dances, songs, chants, music, gestures, body movements, etc. have contributed immensely to the total structuring of the various forms of theatre and that almost the same structural framework has been used in Lai-Haraoba. The important point to be noted in this context is that theatre needs 'an assembled audience' to respond to it. It is the presence of this 'assembled audience' in a ritual which enables us to call that particular ritual a theatre. However, this is not a theatre structured on the Aristotelian model, but a 'drama' composed of songs and dances in which the young and old participate. It is, more or less, a re-enactment of the creation of the Universe through hand movements, dance, songs and incantation, which have become the language of Lai-Haraoba. When the myth of creation is re-enacted it assumes the form of a living theatre. Lai-Haraoba is not an individual writer or artist's work. It has structures which have evolved in the course of long process and a long history in the life of the people. The structure of theatre here is the structure of performance. The text involved is not a written dramatic text, it is the performance text. This is the text perceived by the audience, through the various channels of sensation, produced by the experiences of the actual performance.

Dr. Premchand further elaborates to prove that Lai-Haraoba could be examined as the best example of 'constancy in change' in Manipuri culture. He says that in the history of Manipuri culture, there are various evidences of changes, transformations and synthesis. But, in the midst of all these flux and changes, there is something central or fundamental which has remained constant. This combined phenomenon of change and constancy is very vital to Manipuri culture. It has imparted a distinct identity to Manipuri culture.

The three books, taken together, could give a reader a deep insight into the world of traditional Manipuri culture whose spirit still pervades every leaf of Manipuri cultural life.

REFERENCES

1. Paratt, John and Saroj N. Arambam, *The Pleasing of the Gods*, Vikas Publishing House, New Delhi, 1997.
2. Ratan Kumar, Dr. *Lai-Haraoba of Manipur*, Imphal, 2001.
3. Premchand, Nongthombam: *Rituals and Performance*, Cultural Resource Centre, Imphal, 2005.

6

Pictorial Representation and Knowledge: Case Study of *Hastividyarnava*

Meghali Goswami

I

The idea that pictorial art can have cognitive value, that it can enhance our understanding of the world and of our own selves, has had many advocates in art theory and philosophical aesthetics alike. It has also been argued, that the power of pictorial representation to convey or enhance knowledge, in particular knowledge along with some practical context is not generalized across the medium. Therefore, in "what photography can do" Stephanie Ross argues that non-narrative pictures are confined to appearances, and so cannot promote the kind of understanding necessary for moral and practical knowledge.[1] Pictorial representations in the manuscript carry forward a complete knowledge system, i.e. knowledge of the life—world, nature and the style of the paintings. It is *mimetic* in a special sense beyond its stereotyped nuances.

An artist commonly relies on viewers to draw on their knowledge and experience and, therefore, fills in those aspects of pictorial content that are not being given explicitly. Therefore, for right and proper appreciation pictures need to be informative in the sense that the artist should have some reasons to assume that the prospective viewer will share the knowledge system that the pictures are concerned with. *Hastividyarnava*, depicts a series of events unfolding in time, and therefore has a narrative structure. Such narratives then become vehicles for a specialized knowledge having a didactic character. They help the viewers/readers in appreciating the inner lessons in the representation.

Ross holds that appreciation has to grow from an understanding of the character of the situation, action or event that is being appreciated. It needs to take note of surrounding circumstances and the background condition. To evaluate a certain state of affairs one must understand how the state of affairs came to be; one needs to gain a sense of events causally linked and unfolding in time as different stories yield different evaluations. Art promotes moral and practical knowledge not only in conveying related judgments but mainly in offering justification for the judgments that it conveys in the form of causes, beliefs, and reasons behind the action and events that the judgments are about.

The pictorial narration exploits shared knowledge about the world that it depicts, for instance, the habits, customs, or social relations that it involves, or about the context of presentation. The images are designed with an elaborate working hypothesis about the knowledge relevant to different public domains that anticipated viewers are likely to associate with a picture–for instance, knowledge of society, history, culture, politics, the institution of art or about the system of pictorial representation itself, and the codes and practices that it involves.

The public spheres on which artists draw provide information stock and contextualize the work. Without such contextualization, the meaning of a pictorial representation cannot be encoded. In fact, pictorial representation in manuscripts offers a 'kinetic summary'[2] not for projecting a temporal order or its past but for specifying the very essence or character of the represented state of affairs. It provides information distinctive of the familiar schema of an execution, familiar to contemporary viewers and to viewers of today as well. Hence paintings in manuscript can be looked upon as particular measures for reflecting the continuity of a life-world in such 'kinetic summary', the past is re-enacted here in a live manner. The art activity here has a purpose and a target akin to that of a historian. In assuming a picture under the schema of an execution we move back in time and the past is enlivened in the present. The painting then does not speak of a disjointed fragment of the past but exhibits a holistic history comprising the collective knowledge of people in continuity. It contains within itself the key for its interpretation by viewers.

Paintings in manuscripts are essentially thematic. They are also products of an 'ethnic time', if I am permitted to use this term, the time with its own socio-political and other dimensions. Because of the thematic nature, the titles of these paintings, unlike in the case of the paintings of our time, are of special significance. They unequivocally lead the viewers in the right direction of interpretation. They also render the possibility of reconstructing the narratives by contemporary and future viewers.

Pictorial representation in the sense stipulated here does not function as an autonomous system. Nor is the aesthetic as a self-sufficient category of experience applied here. *Hastividyarnava* is a kind of encyclopaedia the format of which is artistic. It surely has an aesthetic dimension. But, it is not the aesthetic *per se* that constitutes its essence. It is essentially purposive and performs a pedagogic role by transforming the knowledge system regarding fostering and taming elephants, and also, its associated angles. In doing so it envisages a perspective for transferring a specialized form of knowledge and knowledge about its associated life-world from one age to another is reflected in such transference.

One of the most important aspects of the way of life attained by a cultural group is its activity in development of art. On the whole, art is the result of human activities for expressing cultural aspirations. Also, the cultural heritage of a period is in no way separable from the social conditions of the period.

II

In taking the manuscript *Hastividyarnava* as a case study the function of art as a channel of knowledge transmission can be clearly observed. According to Rabindranath Tagore "Art is the response of man's creative soul to the call of the real."[3] Indian art is based on some tradition and temperament. This is reflected in this manuscript. An interpretative understanding of the folios of the manuscript with paintings makes it evident that this manuscript is an important landmark in the history of Assamese literature and painting style.

This manuscript acted as a means for conserving and transmitting culture and learning, representing the artistic sensibilities of the people. The Ahom kings patronized and supported a team of clerks and copyists under the supervision of an officer. This manuscript contains visual illustrations with the subject matter of a treatise on elephant- lore executed under Ambika Devi in 1734 A.D. The author of the treatise, Sukamer Barkath the team leader and Dilbar and Dosai, two Muslim artists from Delhi were the real architects of this literary and artistic monument. There are at present 235 existing folios (the original manuscript had 293 folios). The measurement of each folio is 58cm by 16cm.

The manuscript mentions different species of elephant. It also provides important information about the manners and customs of the people at that time. Thereafter, it also reports about the use of colours in a different manner and technique to paint the tuskers. For the first time artists from outside the region of Assam were employed, whose names were Dilbar and Dosai (from Delhi), to paint the manuscript. Therefore, a totally new style of painting was introduced. The painters added new elements to the paintings, maintaining a strong folk element. In addition, this was for the first time a foreign influence could be traced in this art form – the influence of the Mughal miniatures. About the most remarkable part of the paintings, Basil Gray observes: "Each human, animal and other composition was framed in a kind of architectural niche".[4]

Another remarkable dimension of this manuscript is that the two Muslim artists Dilbar and Dosai were descendents of the Mughal court.[5] Almost in all the folios the depiction of elephants is seen. The painted manuscript gives us valuable information on one hundred and forty eight kinds of tuskers, with their characteristics, modes of training and the natures of their riders. The social aspect of the time is mirrored in the illustrations. For instance, the Royal procession in Mughal style is depicted in detail, showing all attendants accompanying the king according to their positions in the court hierarchy. Royal recreations are also depicted in detail which show performances by musicians and dancers dressed in garbs representing different regions of India. Tussle figures of elephant and buffaloes, the movement of the elephants and their relaxation are skilfully painted.

The architectural settings are painted in such a manner that they look like frames through which the faces of the female figures are painted to suggest that they are enjoying the 'outer' world through the windows and at the same time their royal status. The buildings are painted in a way that they appear to come out of the picture frame. The architecture is suggestive of typical Mughal influence. The folk element was blended with foreign influence for the first time in Assamese folk art.

III

Figure 1 is a folio from the *Hastividyarnava* .The writing in the folio starts with the salutation to Lord Ganesha and Lord Sri Krishna and also mentions the composition of an early work on the subject by Sambhunatha:

> *Pranamya Govinda-padaravindam Sri Sambhunath*
> *Ati Janapratisthita Vivicya Sastrani Puratanani*
> *Gajendra Chintamani Matanoti.*[6]

The painting has no foreground, middle ground or background. The entire folio, where illustration is to be done, is first painted with green and no attempt is made to show the animals in frontal position. The painting depicts the golden deer drinking water and on the left side an attempt is made by the artist to paint the forest from where the deer came out. The second part of the painting shows a herd of elephants. Here it can be mentioned that the artist followed the scroll painting style alongside a continuous narration of the story.[7] Moreover it can be analyzed that the breed of elephant was locally available in Assam and the water element that was painted was perhaps the indication of the local river – the *Brahmaputra* – and these added the folk elements to the painting.

Another folio of the same manuscript traces the stylistic applications of the folk elements. Fig. 2 shows juxtaposition of folk element with the Mughal style. The Mughal influence could be seen in the depiction of the building's architecture as well as of the costumes. Another important reason for introducing Mughal artists was the intense desire of King Rudra Singh for a richer and more sophisticated court life. He was impressed by the life of the princes and nobles in the great cities of Hindustan and introduced these new and varied cultures in Assam. The Mughal dresses consisting of *Pagri, Jame* and *Izar*, which were introduced in Assam, are clearly indicated in the paintings.

As this manuscript was mainly focused on the life of the elephants, elephants were always painted prominently compared to the human figure as seen in Fig 3. This folio describes that an elephant whose body colour is smoky vermilion deserves to be mounted by the King. The manuscript *Hastividyarnava*, predominantly depicts the folk element and no effort to show perspectives and three dimensionality is seen in the illustrations. Also, the human forms show the angularity of the features, the pointed nose, the broad chest and thin waists. The human figures are shown generally short and daintily built.[8]

The female figures are painted as heavy and short compared to their male counterparts. They are gracefully curved; the faces are round and large. The eyes are large and almond shaped or elliptical under highly arched eyebrows and the chins are not prominent. The profusion of hair is bound either in top-knots or in buns at the nape of the neck. The men have small but sharp noses and round staring eyes. The treatment of hands and feet is archaic. The hands are depicted with tapering fingers and the feet are broad and flat. The females are clad in traditional Assamese costume, the *mekhla* and the *chadar*. The *Chadar* comes from behind the neck hanging within the two ends on the chest. Sometimes the *Chadar* or the '*Riha*' (a type of dupatta) is wrapped round the breasts leaving the shoulders bare.[9]

The landscape is reduced to the minimum. The background is usually in monochrome. Sometimes a few plants and flowers is spotted on the ground. The landscape is stylized with trees. The peculiar method of depicting rivers and cloud is all decorative, perhaps symbolic. The paintings had practically no landscaping, the only importance being given was to the human, animal, and architectural elements.[10] Landscape was indicated by applying green colour in some illustrations. Traces of mountains in the background were also indicated.

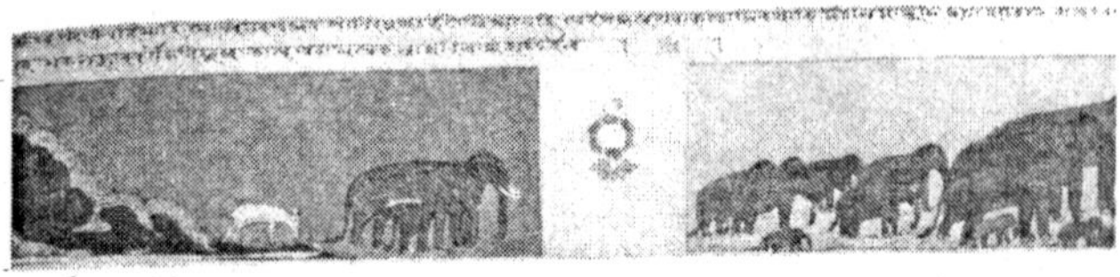

Fig.1: The first script of the folio of the *Hastividyarnava*

Fig.2: Folin from *Hastividyarnava* manuscript describes about the beauty of queen Ambika Devi

Fig.3: Folio from *Hastividyarnava*

Fig.4: Folio from *Hastividyarnava* showsthe rituals performed for the elephants

The architecture in the background is often treated as an outline. The watering surface, rocks etc. are conventionally treated. The human figures and animal figures are shown with forceful postures. The figures are puppet-like. There is lack of expression on the faces which was replaced by the use of *Mudras*.[11] This manuscript was painted under the regional school of painting, the Gargaon School. The technique used by the artist was similar to the Mughal style but was Assamese in spirit. This new style was limited only to the court circle. The style of the manuscripts that follows shows that the paintings were exclusively commissioned by the orders of the royal consorts. It was a matter of great honour for the artists to acknowledge their being selected for the purpose. Also, if observed properly, it is seen that the female figures were painted in a very simple manner with no traces of ornaments on them, which was a contrast with that of the female figures seen in Rajputs, Rajasthani and Mughal minature.[12]

Figure 4 shows the rituals that they practiced; the importance of the priest in the society and also the simplicity of the female living in that place, showing very strong folk elements. If noticed properly, the second part of the figure shows the painting of the *mandala*, - the full bloom eight petal lotus, which was purely a *'Tantric'* symbol. This kind of paintings was also available in the manuscripts of Nepal.[13] Through this part of the painting it was clear that *Tantrism* was practiced by the people of Assam since long. The upper part of the painting shows that rituals for the elephants also were performed. Choudhury points out that the paintings show the performance of *Puja* according to some folk traditions .[14]

IV

To conclude, it can be said that people belonging to a region or a cultural milieu are noted for their particular form of life. The different aspects of their way of life reveal the extent of civilization attained by the people concerned. One of the most important aspects of the way of life attained by a cultural group is its achievement in development of art. In a broad sense, art covers all the phenomena which are the outcomes of the exercise of human ingenuity as directly opposed to 'nature'.

Theodor Adorno declared that art is a form of knowledge.[15] In a somewhat similar vein, his critical theorist colleague Herbert Marcuse characterized art as a mode of cognition that is an alternative to positivism. Both Adorno and Benjamin think of art as a form of language, [16] or having a language-like character, which incites philosophical reflection.[17] The discussion of art as a form of pictorial knowledge, and having a language-like character can therefore be clearly traced in the *Hastividyanarva* manuscript.

The textual tradition like that of *Hastividyarnava* speaks for the value of a special kind of mimesis. It is not mere representation or mimesis in its stereotyped sense of imitation. It is a unique blend of words and images with the purpose of mirroring a life-world. Inadequacy of words minus images and images minus words is met with the help of this blend. The concept of mimesis is explicable here in the range and depth of the issues that are cognitive, psychological, ethical and cultural.[18] *Hastividyarnava* is a tradition, transmission of which over the ages to future generations is possible for its mimetic nature in this particular sense of representation or *mirroring a life-world* for carrying forward the details of a form of life.

REFERENCES

1. Ross, www. Archnet.com\photography cited 16th Nov. 2008.
2. Nochline, www.artstudy.org.in, cited 14th Sept. 2008.
3. Tagore, R.N., 1978, *Angel of Surplus,* Visva Bharati, Calcutta
4. Gray, Basil., 1953, The Development of Paintings in India in the 16th Century, *Marg,* Vol. No. 3, Bombay, p 20.
5. Ahmed, K, 1994, *The Art and Architecture of Assam,* Spectrum Publications,Guwahati.
6. Goswami, H., 1930, *Descriptive Catalogue of Assamese Manuscripts,* Calcutta University, p.xxvi.
7. Gait., Sir Edward, 1963, *A History of Assam,* Calcutta, 3rd ed., p.16.
8. Goswami. H, 1917, *The Darrang Raj Vansavali,* Calcutta.
9. Das Gupta, R.,1972, *Eastern Indian Manuscript Painting.* D.B. Tharaporevala Sons & Co. Pvt. Ltd., Bombay, p. 2.
10. Choudhary,C.P. 1976, *Hastividyarnava,* N. K Gossain & Co (Pvt), Ltd., Calcutta. p. iv.

11. Das Gupta, R., 1972, *Eastern Indian Manuscript Painting*. D.B. Tharaporevala Sons Co. Pvt. Ltd., Bombay, p. 2.

12. Choudhary,C, P, 1976, *Hastividyarnava*, N. K Gossain & Co.(Pvt), Ltd., Calcutta. p. iv.

13. *Ibid.*, p. iv.

14. *Ibid.*, p. iv.

15. Adorno, T. 1997. *Aesthetic Theory* (R. Hullot-Kentor, Trans.). Minneapolis: University of Minnesota. (Original work published 1970).

16. Benjamin, W. 1997c. *Theory of Knowledge*. In M. Bullock, M., & M. Jennings, (eds.), *Selected Writings*.

17 Marcuse, H. 1998. *Eros and Civilization: A philosophical inquiry into Freud*. London: Routledge.(Original work published 1955).

18. Halliwell, Stephen. 2002, *The Aesthetic of Mimesis*, Princeton University Press, Princeton and Oxford, p.13.

7

The Performance of Identity and Histories of Representation

Rimli Bhattacharya

Politically volatile since (and before) Independence, and geographically isolated from most of the subcontinent, particularly after Partition, the region which now passes homogenously in popular discourse as 'the Northeast', is I argue simultaneously represented for mainstream India in 'performances' of ethnicity. For many Indians even today, the major part of the north-eastern region of the subcontinent is perceived as remote, exotic, tribal and so on. A region whose borders are shared with China, Bhutan, Myanmar, in later times, East Pakistan, now Bangladesh, perhaps lends itself easily to many of these epithets.

The paper attempts to outline the complex, often contradictory, nature of the politics of difference and identity formation, particularly as articulated in the media and in academia, by invoking multiple histories of the region in sites *other than* within the boundaries of the 'northeast'. This is not to deny the shared histories of migration of peoples, overlap of languages, of geographical and political isolation or the oppression of different societies within this region, and their largely contestary relationship with the state. However, a synoptic plotting of specific cultural practices is intended to raise critical questions about the spaces for representation and revitalisation available to us today. And thereby to raise a few questions on the nature of cultural practice itself, I coin the term 'unbounding' to refer to this project.

Preamble

A word perhaps about the disciplinary perspectives that shape my concerns, which in turn continue to be challenged and realised in praxis. Work in primary education (creating teaching material, evaluating textbooks and workshops with teachers) in various parts of the country, including Assam and Bengal, informs to a large extent my understanding of the politics of language and education. My research into performance histories has required me to be wary of formulating anything like a linear connection between oral and print cultures.[1] Similarly, one is alerted to the complexities of region, language and representation in the process of syllabus revision while devising an inter-disciplinary framework within the discipline of English Literature in India. Above all, the daily experience of teaching and interacting with students from various parts of north-eastern India at the University of Delhi provides a contemporary interrogative edge to established 'truths'. All of these find resonances of absence and presence of course, in my own childhood and adolescence in Assam.

Yet none of these facts or factors is sufficiently compelling or overarching enough by itself to alert one to the changing perceptions of self and the other, group and collective, that I seek to map here. This essay then, while firmly located in the present, seeks to focus on select markers of identity which have consolidated themselves in either popular memory and/or through institutional practices, only some of which are state funded or otherwise supported.

My paper draws in part on two companion pieces presented some six years ago.[2] One of them, 'Performance and Ethnicity: Towards Contextualising the "Northeast" in India' was conceived as a collage working through juxtaposition. Much of the irony that emerged from cuts, freezes and inter-titles in that presentation is inevitably lost in a paper that is written up. I would nevertheless urge the reader to view the sections that follow in the representational mode of a collage to uncover an ongoing intellectual argument.

I shall only be able to gesture at the second of these pieces which involved a close reading of two stories written at my request by one of my former MA students. Himself a Tanghkul Naga from the Ukhrul district of Manipur[3], the writer (Varseo Ningshen) was also implicitly exploring his own location as outsider-insider to the region and the supernatural crux of his tales in relation to his Christian beliefs. The stories were thus much more than exercises in retelling legends in English.[4]

Rethinking Territories

As mentioned, I shall be proposing a thesis of 'unbounding' the region—whether defined linguistically, or by political boundaries which are constructed, contested and ever prone to reshaping or fragmentation. Some substantial efforts have been made in this direction, requiring us to rethink of borders as porous, settlements and habitats as formed or un-formed by migration, displacement and so on, and of colonial imperatives in missions of religion, revenues and labour. In speaking of the 'birth' of the Lushai Hills through colonial intervention, historian Indrani Chatterjee points out:

> I can only refer readers to older chronicles of neighboring kingdoms of Sylhet, Tripura, Cachar, Manipur, Burma, Assam and Chittagong all of which claimed parts of these hills at various times between the 17th and 19th centuries. The region was fashioned into a 'borderland' only gradually through the nineteenth century.[5]

The title of Chatterjee's essay, 'Slaves, Souls and Subjects in *a South Asian Borderland*' (emphasis mine) foregrounds the making of certain kinds of subjecthood, often through erasures of nuances within languages[6] and of other shared resources. But the perspective is also of an extended geographical domain, in this case, 'South Asian', with an emphasis of the mutability of borders.

I choose therefore to argue against the notion of cultural identity as either given or fixed and consequently easily available, or at least recoverable—whether for display (for others) as ethnicity or for a less public process of internalisation. Authenticity, rootedness, heritage and originary moments are valued as constituting distinctive ethnicity as much as they do in discourses of nationalism. By extension, they operate critically on founding claims for self-determination not only against the 'mainstream' but inevitably against other minority claims of ethnicities. The last century in particular has shown us the unfortunate consequences of being trapped in these limited possibilities. This is all the more tragic given the actual nature of uneven development or unequal rights that in fact generates legitimate claims for a selfhood.

The claims of exclusive difference then is not necessarily a one-way process, but is often conferred from without, whether for short term bargaining gains by a partisan state, or by the ostensibly objective parameters of a discipline. The 'limitation' of perspectives arising from disciplinary orientations are perhaps the more difficult to identify and confront. It is not surprising that much of the literatures and performance forms from northeastern India continue to be studied under the rubric of 'folklore' or the 'traditional'. (This is of course equally the case with other regions, e.g. Purulia in contemporary West Bengal, or Bastar in Madhya Pradesh and so on.) It is not surprising for instance, that a majority of students in my M.Phil. seminars choose to work with the folktale. In doing so, there is rarely if ever a contestation of the available structures of narrative theory, whether of formalist origin or from a more specifically anthropological basis. The terms of reference would appear to be already available within or impressed upon the site marked out for study.

In addition, historically, the nature of education (both content and pedagogy) in post-Independent India has for most part continued with alienating modes of relating to the object of study. Post-colonialism taken at its least rigorous has given us back the 'native informant', without the ghost of a chance to identify or make visible our colonising selves. This is a statement I would apply across literatures and cultures, operating with a particular strategic intent in academia in the first and third worlds.

Is it possible then to move out of this boundedness, as it were, and offer alternative narratives which move through history and yet address the particular complex and fluid realities of our present location? Unbounding may be interpreted as an active critical process of historicising through juxtaposition. The narrative thus engendered would at best constitute a counter-narrative, in which the subjective is privileged, as is the subject, at any given moment.

Modes of Exchange

In the study of visual cultures the focus has shifted from performance to *reception*; I am personally interested in the movement of images, of practices, their interpretation and reconfiguration, through a negotiation of shared traits and difference. Issues of reception become critical in case of minority or marginal groups, who are often forced to cast themselves in the mould most acceptable, or most likely to be funded by the State or by the market, and increasingly, a combination of the both. The global market in the early 21st century is celebratory of difference as multiculturalism. This, I would argue, makes for very predictable and extremely limited modes of expressivity, both at the individual and collective level. In some instances the potential patron/consumer is persuaded to believe in a contradiction: viz. that the 'product' is unique because it is so different as to be beyond one's ken; as well as that it is different only superficially; the process of bringing it to the patron/consumer has already made it not merely accessible, but 'same'. At both levels the loss is in the delight of the unfamiliar, the grappling with signification, and the investment of the self as a continuous and not one-off encounter.

Might there be some enabling questions which allow for a shift of focus? How for instance, might one begin to theorise questions of ethnicity in a *metropolitan* context, beginning perhaps within the colonial metropolitan? For, the imbrication of the metropolis serves at least two immediate purposes: firstly, in the case of Calcutta, considered 'The Second City of the Empire' in colonial times, research has by and large focussed on 'Bengali culture' in which other linguistic or ethnic groups do not figure in any significant way. For example, few historians of Bengali theatre have taken into account the dominant presence of Parsi theatre in the city during the golden age of the public theatre. Secondly, the metropolitan location is ostensibly more outward looking and plays host to cosmopolitan impulses. It draws not only resident populations (whether merchants, traders or labourers) but its superior network of educational, legal, and cultural infrastructure as also the accumulation of capital in the hands of indviduals (even if through absentee landlordism) invites bodies of student populations from neighbouring regions, as also seasonal migrations of performers from distant places, from all across the far-flung British Empire. And further, coming to the present, in a metropolis such as Delhi (more properly the NCT or National Capital Region) which is itself expanding rapidly if unevenly in the context of a globalised economy, the possibility of playing host is given a tremendous boost by the actual location of the Centre, the nation-state's government. A vast investment is made through staging participatory forms of cultural differences—as material, people and crafts—in specific sites. In the last decade, 'the north-east' has been the predominant locus of this investment.

I should add that at least in some of the illustrations with which I respond to the above questions, neither 'ethnic' nor 'folk' or 'tribal' may have been *consciously* used in the construction of an identity. I am also suggesting a projection of identity on the part of those who consider themselves as outside of these categories. Thus for example, while none of the terms mentioned earlier *appears* to be critical in the construction of 'Bengaliness'; arguably, they are operative in stabilising a shared understanding of 'bhadralok culture'. This is addressed briefly in the first of the routes I trace.

The second route moves along the axes of the festival, in its many historical reimaginings. They include ticketed performance, entry with passes to state or corporate sponsored events, or the festival as participatory marking the seasonal and /or ritual calendar and the everyday. None of these are mutually exclusive, in fact, they are often overlapping. The festival in particular encourages the idealisation of a community, especially when it becomes the state's agenda to grant finance and authenticity. My aim would be to understand the community as it defines itself in these select moments, and where possible, to delineate the politics of location.

Manipur[7]/Manipuri

Professor Joychandra Singh's paper presented at the seminar makes it clear that the *lai haraoba* is accepted as constituting a certain unique and 'foundational' feature of Manipuri identity which traces a history from 33 CE to mid-19th century.[8] Even the glimpses that were possible within the confines of a seminar paper (rather than through one's own participation in the haraoba), makes evident the centrality of celebration in the term *haraoba*—invoking festival, festivities, the celebration of generation, the imagery of life-giving rains. The specialised and the demotic nature of the festival, or should I say festivals, is indeed often the domain of the ritual. It is also the site where the self-constructed ethnic subject is most prone to turning inwards the anthropological gaze.

A possible question here is that of conveying this centrality (as a distinctive cultural marker) to other audiences? Even if one moved out print culture, degraded digitised images (as is the case more often than not) may be neither more real or participatory.

Keeping this question in abeyance, one may make a metaphor of the practice of *jhum* (swidden) cultivation, and consider a narrative of shifting contexts. This would be specifically though not exclusively relevant in the case of performance. Therefore, rather than examining 'the thing itself' my focus is on the modalities of representation, the discourse around performance (which to a great extent determines the 'transaction' or the 'translation' taking place) and the investment of significance and of meaning thereof. As Jyotindra Jain points out in his introductory essay to a recent study of image mobility in India's popular culture: 'The social meaning and value of a cultural object [and practice] may be located in its human transactions, through its historical circulation...a processual approach, the emphasis being placed on mobility and migration.'[9]

I shall take 'the dancer and the dance' as one of the many possible strands we may take up for examination. One reason for doing so would be to deconstruct the 'naturalness' of dance in relation to the category tribe or folk. The definition of 'tribe' in one of the amendments of the Constitution of India, as cited in KS Singh: 'those fond of drinking and dancing'[10] (But which of us is not?!).

The circulation of the referent 'Manipuri' in relation to dance yields a heterogeneous harvest in the context of colonial Bengal to the present time. The multiple representations include epithets such as respectable, royal, professional (as in working for money), exotic, foreign. It is worth emphasising that the dancers—obviously a different set at various historical junctions—are introduced into the long tradition of anti-theatrical diatribe in Bengal. This latter history spanning a century and a half foregrounds the question of gender and sexuality in/through performance of the streets as well as on stage. It is discursively linked with 'news' 'opinions' 'reports' and the like to a print culture that was at least bilingual, if not multilingual, and active in metropolitan (Calcutta) or semi-metropolitan locations (Dhaka).

For want of space I begin by selectively juxtaposing two such media reports:

> *Time: 1820s* *Location: Calcutta*
>
> First, a 'Manipur jatra troupe' performs in the drawing room of the rich Calcutta bania Motilal Seal in 1826, with women playing the role of Krishna. The *Samachar Darpan* of 19 August 1826 records that the performers were slighted by the audience on 'aesthetic grounds'.[11] The report is sourced from a period when the drawing rooms of the Indian comprador class of old and new landowners, of dewans, banias and others offering services as agents to the Company attracted novelties from diverse places. The seasonal migration of baijis and tawaiifs from different parts of India fed into the steady stream of 'nautch' performances for the new elite and the English merchants, administrators, officers.
>
> *Time: 1890s* *Location: Dhaka*
>
> The second cluster is culled from towards the end of the century from a [necessarily selective] exchange in print.[12] Note the sarcasm with which the *Dhaka Prakash* reports on what is perceived as the double standards of the Brahmos who were by and large hostile to the public theatre.[13] (Print apart, the hostility was made manifest in student demonstrations, public meetings, picketing and so on.)

In the following report the '*bideshi nartakis*' or foreign dancers are located in an elite space of consumption for the select few. They are used to score a point in the morality debate around public performance and the *beshya-abhinetri*.[14] The construction of sexualities, male and female, is the site of debate.

News

Last Tuesday night, at the house of Babu Rajanikanta Ghosh—that ideal of Brahmos, saw the completion of the auspicious programme of the Manipuri dancers. Many model Brahmos and Brahmikas participated in this pure activity. These were those very same people who had been so incensed at the local/indigenous [deshiya] dancers for performing in *Bibah Bibhrat natak*, that they had vowed to never ever see the faces of the latter. We were quite delighted to find them breaking their vow on account of the superiority of these *bideshi* dancers, and for the sports and tricks of those barely clad women who perform in circuses.

23 March 1893, *Dhaka Prakash*[15]

News

The performance of *Purnachandra Natak* has commenced once again, after a run of *Chaitanya Lila* at the Crown Theatre in Patuatuli. We were immensely pleased after witnessing a performance the other day. Those who raise objections [to the theatre] on the ground that these are enchanting prostitutes performing in the above piece may well deprive themselves of the beauty and pleasure of performance. In a situation when the common public is not in a position to witness respectable ladies singing and dancing; when it is not possible for them to have respectable Manipuri lady dancers give them pleasure through their daily performances; and when, lacking these alternatives, people are obliged to join the song and dance events by *bais* and *khemtawalis*, we do not consider that it is wrong for anyone to attend the above play, which is infinitely superior to the latter. It is true that the play lacks the amateurishness of respectable ladies, of songs sung out of tune; the play is also completely lacking in the gestures and provocative play of the bais and khemtawalis. But it abounds in the modesty of bhadramahilas, and combines the musical skills of the baiwalis with the khemtawali's sport, just as it has pleasing costumes, and moral counsel on the consequences of song and dance. If we agree that we must have pleasure and entertainment then, it is our duty to enjoy them in this manner.

21 May 1893, *Dhaka Prakash*[16]

However, the Manipuri dancers must have gone public not long before this, for a review of their performance at the Crown Theatre the very next month was extremely positive, although couched in the usual superior patronising tone of bhadra discourse.

Anyway, the extended review of 2 April 1893 in the same newspaper discloses that the dancers were from 'the royal family' and brought on a tour 'at his own expense' by a certain Mr GC Ganguli 'originally from Bikrampur and now residing in Manipur, for holding performances in Calcutta and Dhaka.' To summarise this long review: the performers are praised on aesthetic grounds, for their mastery of *taan-laya*, their brilliant *abhinaya*, and the costumes. Of the language, it is noted that while in general 'the foreign is barbaric', in this instance, the presence of Bangla and Braj bhasha redeems this barbarity to some extent. Finally, attention is drawn to a novel spectacle—of the women dancing as 'Naga braves'.

This particular juxtaposition only offers a partial unbounding; an access to alternative accounts/histories of the same event is still missing. What for instance, were the imperatives that made the tour possible or necessary or desirable in the first place? What kind of trade or other contacts were already in place in the regions we are looking at? To what extent was this mediated through Vaishnavism, in particular Meitei Vaishnavism? What have been the role of dancers in the royal family in Manipur? What was Mr Ganguli's role/location as a cultural mediator? On what basis did the Brahmos organise the event in Dhaka? In short, there is a rich vein of archival history that has to be tapped and unearthed *from multiple sources*. My argument gestures towards this possibility, focussing, as I have said at the beginning of this paper, on the reception context, i.e. the complexity of factors that determine reception. Theatre in Bengal was a particularly fraught site for evoking strong polemics and postions, with the actress or the female performer as a nodal point. The circulation of 'Manipuri' then, in the instances cited above is almost entirely in relation to the ongoing debate on morality. Although, some appreciation is meted out on 'aesthetic' grounds, they are understood in relation to a standard of *taan-laya* etcetera by which 'Manipuri' has to pass a test.

One could complement this history with that of the referent 'Bengali' in Manipur and among Manipuris. Lokendra Arambam's exegesis of what he calls 'The Manipur Experience' in relation to modernism in theatre, gives us glimpses of the what we today speak of as forms of 'internal colonisation'. After Manipur becomes a part of the British Empire in 1891, Arambam traces the continuing anti-British statements to the 'ushering in of a colonial economy, when absolutely different racial categories, notablv the Marwaris and the Bengalis were foisted upon the new social structure organised under colonial principles.'[17] Not only are Bengalis (the educated Babus) the 'new resource persons for colonial education' but it marks the entry of proscenium theatre into Manipur. The Victoria Club of 1903 'was a landmark in the beginnings of proscenium arched theatre' ... and 'plays from Hindu mythology were the main attractions.'

Time: 1920s *Location: Santiniketan*

> We next move in time to an experimental space conceptualised as a nursery for the new Indian subject. The original brahmacharya ashram modelled after 'ancient' ideals soon begins to extend itself in hitherto unimagined ways. Here, performance, as in song and later, dance, is woven into the everyday. Rabindranath Tagore envisions in the learning environment of Santiniketan, particularly after the founding of Visva-Bharati, the possibility of drawing on multiple traditions, forging individuated cultural idioms, not specifically bound by markers of gender, caste or region.

What did 'Manipuri' mean to the multiple cultural streams that were invited to flow into and through the dusty red soil of Birbhum, in the enclave of Santiniketan? How would one relate this inflow specifically to the idiom of dance that, as I have argued elsewhere, was central to Tagore's concept of *utsav* as it evolved in Santiniketan? Why, particularly in the case of dance, were performances not confined to Santiniketan, but involved regular ticketed shows in the neighbouring metropolis, Calcutta, and eventually to the entire subcontinent? In what ways did 'Manipuri nritya' travel to other parts of India? Clearly, the topic merits a study in itself. The emphasis here will be to suggest a few implications of this voyage, the focus will be on the impulses/imperatives informing Tagore's praxis in Santiniketan, rather than exploring in detail the nature of those performances.

The invitation to Boddhimanta Singh to Santiniketan in 1920 was the beginning of a long and tortuous breach into Bengali bhadralok sensibilities which could only regard a girl or woman from a bhadra family dancing as an anathema. Tagore became the butt of vitriolic attacks in print for thus exposing young girls to the public gaze.[18] The introduction of the 'Manipuri' in this context is significant on several counts. The exchange was facilitated through a personal friendship with the ruler of Tripura, Birendramanikya, whose court favoured a Bengalicised culture.

However, Tagore appears not so much interested in the possibility of importing *in toto* an authentic or essentialised 'manipuri' culture, as he is in making available to a new generation of Indians the riches/resources from diverse cultures within and without the subcontinent. His own extensive travels in the subcontinent and abroad and his desire to witness the performative traditions of other cultures initiated the movements of artists and their art forms into Santiniketan.

As I have argued elsewhere, for Tagore, it was the exploration for a feminine sensibility in *both* men and women (as opposed to muscular imperialism), to be realised in the everyday life of Santiniketan and Visvabharati, that greatly impelled his involvement in dance and the training of young girls. The weaving together of songs in movement, with 'pauses' of verse embedded in the plays,[19] offered an altogether new idiom of representation and participation. The form and lyrical idiom of the *nritya natya* or dance-dramas, as they came to be called, made possible a fusion of eastern sensibilities of femininity and of perfomance forms. The 'East' in this case of course encompassed swathes of Southeast Asia and East Asia as well as Bengal's immediate eastern neighbours, specifically, Manipur. It is to be noted that the successive decades saw a steady inflow of teachers from different parts of the subcontinent: Kerala Kalamandalam (Vallathol), Gujarat, extending to Kandy, *as well as* from extended south and south-east Asia, notably, Bali and Java.

What then could 'the festive' or 'a festival' mean in the early decades of the twentieth century as the original brahmacharya ashram school of Santiniketan finds itself moulting into 'Visva-bharati'? The chosen name enshrines the manifesto: here the world may come to nest. The affirmative thrust was on supporting a community-in-formation in a desacralised world, in a *desh* still colonised.[20]

Tagore's long engagement with Vaishnavism notwithstanding, the invitation to Manipuri in Santiniketan emerges as much from a search for form for his own expressive works (poetry, plays, evolving into the nritya-natya) as it does from freeing the body, male and female, from an oppressive regime of regulation on the one hand, and as an alternative to that which is considered vulgar—professional actresses dancing in the public theatre.

It would be worth tracing, but beyond the scope of this essay, how 'Manipuri nritya' figures in the writings of Pratima Devi or Santideb Ghose, two important practitioners who have recorded the evolution of dancing days of the ashram. For reasons of space I offer a few vignettes from two of the latter's works.[21]

1. When the initial training of boys (aged 8 and above) began Tagore also persuaded some of the younger teachers to join. 'But anxious about drawing unfavourable criticism *(birup samalochanar ashonkaye)* at the news of teaching the schoolboys to dance in those days, the monthly newsletter of the school, Santiniketan' had to couch it as 'instruction in *musical drill*' *(sangeetik byam shiksha)* (emphasis mine) taught by two artists from the court of Tripura.[22]

2. The actual process of training often involved learning selected aspect of a dance form, but primarily meant adaptations of diverse dance movements to the text (and songs in question). For example, a mix of Manipuri, Kathakali, Kandyan dance along with Indian folk dances was incorporated into the various movements of *Shapmochan*.

3. *Bōls*, or pure rhythm oriented movements were incorporated into the bhavas of different songs. This, the expressive content carried by the poetry, and to some extent the *sur*, determined the choreography. There are also instances as when the dancer Nabakumar composes an interlude of *bōl* to be danced in the pauses of the song,[23] or when a song was composed to the rhythm of a particular tala.[24] Manipuri dancing also became *integral* to the programmes celebrating the Bengali new year (Poila Boishakh).[25]
4. Santidev as a teacher and dancer was adventurous enough to engage in intensive residential visits to distant Kerala (the poet Vallathol's Kalamandalam) on the one hand and to Imphal on the other (in 1933); for the latter he had to get a special permit.[26]
5. 'The training in music and dances ... did not follow any syllabus fixed by ordinances and examinations; it was based on the needs of various functions and festivals....But from 1935 Gurudev introduced regular study of dances from Manipur and Kerala.'[27]
6. In 1929, Ambalal Sarabhai, impressed by performances of Natir Puja and Nataraj invites Nabakumar Singh to come to Ahmedabad to train his daughters in dancing. Subsequently, he went to Bombay in 1935 to teach Manipuri dancing there.[28]

Time: 1935 *Location: Calcutta*

In 1935, the mainstream Bengali magazine *Desh* carried a column on the arrival of dancers, about 20 in number, from Manipur (men and women) on a tour arranged by the well-known impressario Haren Ghosh. 'They will perform only the *real* nritya of Manipur...which has so overwhelmed Vishwakobi Rabindranath...'[29] (emphasis mine). Here, the mediation is through the seal of Tagore' approval. We do not miss the irony of the furore caused by dancing in Santiniketan and elsewhere under the auspices of Tagore, which is completely missing in this item.

The same issue carried a column on Uday Shankar's troupe which was then touring Lahore, Delhi, Kanpur, Lucknow, Allahabad, Baranasi, Patna and was to perform in the Empire

Theatre at Calcutta. In this instance, it is Shankar and his company who are perceived as a curiosity: *tahara nrityakhela pradarshan koribe,* they will be exhibiting their dances. Uday Shankar had come from abroad to present 'Indian' dance as it had been painstakingly evolved by him and various other improvisators.

Time: 1980-90s *Location: Imphal*

alienation isolation integration pluralistic roots tribal authentic

These are some of the keywords that emerge from special issue of *Seagull Theatre Quarterly* (1997) dedicated to theatre in Manipur.

An excerpt from an interview with playwright Lokendra Aramban poses an additional dimension to those already outlined—of text and authorship.

> In 1987 I did a work based on Tagore's *Raja*—I did the play *in the tribal idiom,* expressing Tagore's emotion, the Raja's quest, alienation and God's existence. It was badly received by the purists of Santiniketan. ...I hadn't put anything of Tagore in it, *except the vital theme which affected us*....anyway, seven years later I wanted to do *Macbeth*...because I have dealt with issues of violence, ritual murder and tragedy. So I wanted to interpret Shakespeare from *my own tribal tradition*. (emphases mine)[30]

'The purists of Santiniketan' need only to look back at the history of invitation experimentation and assimilation that proved a source of vitality in the early decades of Santiniketan, glimpses of which have been shown above. There is a profound irony of 'protecting' or 'guarding' this legacy from precisely the same process in later times. Arambam's comment finds an echo in the long-time resident of Santiniketan, the eminent artist and scholar KG Subramaniyam who does not flinch from mentioning how the theatrical experiments of the legendary painter and sculptor Ramkinkar Baij were interfered with and thwarted by 'the local cultural popes'![31]

Time: 1990s *Location: Calcutta and suburbs, Bankura...*

Dance has been central to Kumar Shahani's films from the very first feature, *Maya Darpan* (1972) in which he collaborated with Chandralekha, working with Mayurbhanj Chau. The 'organisation of the camera movement for cinemascope in relation to the human body found its inspiration from Kudiyattam' in his film *Tarang* (1983).[32] Kelucharan Mahapatra and Odissi, the dancer, the dance weave in and out of the mise-en-scene of *Bhavantara* (1991) and *Bamboo Flute* (1999). In wanting to make a film of Tagore's last novel *Char Adhaya*, Shahani chose to extend the poet's deep involvement with painting which had begun late in his life. The novel (novella really) is conceived in imagistic terms, almost as synaesthetic 'movements'. Colour is evoked in strands and impressions.

Working on and in this film (both as a script consultant and later as a production coordinator) afforded an initiation in the realisation of a film, at a conceptual and material level. Movement and gesture signified more than grace, in every sense of the word. K.K. Mahajan's camera movement and lighting choreographed the terror and pity of the protagonists' passion. Their entrapment in the coils of what passed as nationalism, the violence which destroyed one's self, *swadharma*.

Shahani chose to approach Debjani Chaliah who is a practitioner and teacher of Manipuri dance. She is herself from Assam but has spent much of her life in Calcutta, working sometimes in collaboration with artists and choreographers from institutions in Manipur.[33] Shahani's 'cue' was brief and somewhat enigmatic: movements of animals, movement representing animals and a choregraphy working with these abstracted movements.

I direct my reflections to one outdoor shot that is conceived in sharp contrast to the labyrinth of colonial mansions and classical columns, the almost stifling plant life of many greens and the relentless weight of words which activate memory and loss in the film.

Ela the heroine is seated on an ornate cast iron bench we encounter elsewhere in the film, again in lush green surroundings, water nearby. Next to her is Indranath, to whom she has been drawn—as a leader, a messiah almost.

In the film this is a moment when Ela and Indranath are seated on the same bench apparently oblivious of each other. Three young women in white dressed (not as Radha or Krishna), moving in and out of the camera's frame, sinuous, supple and lyrical. But the overwhelming *effect* is one of sinister grace, of power abstracted.

The evocation of this sequence through the rest of the film is ripple-like, working with light and water in shots which are more pronouncedly along a vertical axis. Even so the movement of the dark half uncoiled hair and dark skin tone of one of the dancers with the stark white drapery, 'Manipuri' is not fetishised. A new configuration of stylised dance movements (themselves internalised in years of disciplinary training) is found for the film. 'Santiniketani' as it circulates in popular bhadralok metropolitan, suburban and diasporic cultural exhibitions is eschewed. This too, would offend cultural purists and popes, guardians of regional ethnicities of whatever provenance.

Choosing to privilege the relationship between movement, material and medium, I quote Shahani on cinematography: 'KK was not just a cameraman. Through KK and his assistants, even the trolley pushers, the choreography gets a different relationship to the dancers and to the trees and nature around them. The body of the cameraman in relation to his lens brings into the film an unexplored dimension of a much rehearsed movement.'[34]

ARCHIVES OF THE FUTURE?[35]
The Republic Day Parade

This section addresses questions of circulation in relation to spaces (physical and ideological) that are already assigned, as it were: parades, displays, opening and closing ceremonies, state-funded festivals and so on. This may also include events or celebrations intended to bring together groups of people under a common nomenclature, signalling resistance to a hegemonic other, usually the nation-state.

Almost throughout 1952, Prime Minister Jawaharlal Nehru (who was concerned about this integration of post-Independence India with voices of dissent emerging from culturally diverse regions) engaged himself in giving shape to the cultural pageant, comprising tableaux of folk and tribal life and dance forms, to be inculcated into the Parade.

Jyotindra Jain argues that 'the visual archives of the Republic Day Parades not only fed their own growth over 55 years but significantly began to provide the standard for authentic cultural behaviour, self/image formation, and the construction of identity back in the village and in tribal communities.'[36]

The paradigm of regional-national/international is thus recontextualised not only in the questioning of the national, but in the fundamental claim of a return to a pre-colonial independence different from that of other princely states in the Indian sub-continent.

In a situation where about 50 Naga tribes are spread all over the region, extending into Myanmar and a complex history of Burmese and British imperialism, the civilizing mission of Christianity and Revivalism. Both Revivalism and Rock and Roll have a place in representation of ethnicity and Christianity during the celebration of the Naga National Reconciliation. The *North East Sun,* a lively magazine in English and popular amongst students living elsewhere in the country, carried a report with photographs in 2002: More than 10,000 Nagas assembled where items of the mass performance included the stitching together of tribal shawls, the burning of (Indian) currency and singing along with the songs of Bob Dylan.[37]

In December 2009, a feature article in *The Hindu* (definitely more mainstream than *The North East Sun*) reports on the annual Hornbill festival organised by the State government of Nagaland, 'as a veritable showcase of Naga life'. The writer continues: 'With tourism and preservation of Naga culture [already a question here in the combination of the two] as the topmost agenda of this annual affair, the Morung's exhibition is central to the festival. At the Naga heritage village, the morungs of 16 different Naga tribes....were replicated in the same way "as per the inhabited areas of Nagaland. So a viewer is being taken to the actual tribal belts" as put by Khekiye K. Sema, commissioner and secretary, Nagaland.'[38]

But even this 'surreal' conveyor belt glimpses of heritage are undercut by the ground reality of neighbouring Korea (I assume the South) as an important model for the youth by way of films and fashion.

'The Hornbill festival held in the first week of December shows that with its stunning natural beauty and great cultural traditions, Nagaland can offer a rich fare to tourists.'

'The 20-lakh-strong Naga people, by nature, are fun lovers, and life in Nagaland is one long festival.'

'For encouraging inter-tribal cultural interaction and bringing together the festivals of the various tribes under one umbrella, the Government of Nagaland has evolved a festival called the Hornbill festival where one can see a melange of Naga cultural displays at one place. Organised by the State Directorate of Tourism every year between December 1 and 5 in Kohima since 2000, the festival is intended to revive, protect and preserve the richness and uniqueness of the Naga heritage and attract tourists.'[39]

The above quotations from another serious article in the magazine *Frontline* point to a similar process at work: of introducing a number of tribes (spread in different regions including abroad) under a common umbrella of the Hornbill festival.

If we move away from the difficulty of refraining from stereotypes in print, how may we consider events in metropolitan contexts in which there is a degree of participation.

The Tokhu Emong 2007 festival with the motto: 'Igniting a colorful heritage' was organised by the Kyong Welfare Forum. The word kyong apparently means people; the specific tribe is the Lotha, considered one of the most progressive amongst the Nagas. The Chief Guest is Professor Omprakash Mishra, PVC of IGNOU and a Brigadier who is the Deputy Director General, Territorial Army, the Guest of Honour. Mishra has begun a new programme at IGNOU on the Northeast for 'those who desire to know more about the region'. Part of India's 'Look East' policy, the centrality of the Northeast acknowledged, an important role, a responsible player in tomorrow's India.

Clearly arising from a geo-political strategy and a new policy of 'mainstreaming', with the belated recognition that the onus is as much on the 'mainlanders' as it is on those living in the region. Perhaps China's growing might and the fairly well-known porous borders existing in parts of Arunachal, Manipur, Mizoram and Nagaland where trading in all kinds of goods (including perhaps arms and drugs) is done in RMB, Chinese currency, rather than Indian. The Brigadier stressed his friendship with the 'eminent people' of Dimapur, but referred to the festival as 'the new year'.

Stephen, who introduced the festival, repeatedly used the word 'forefathers' in conjunction with the 'thanksgiving' festival in his bilingual speech. He spoke of 'the many cultural gains that can enrich us' through the celebration, which was also a time for exchanging gifts.

The stage was decorated with strips of woven cloth (*mekhala*, shawl and other garments), now rarely used by the members of the audience, except perhaps on occasions such as this. A couple of baskets and three bead necklaces (courtesy the Nagaland emporium on Baba Kharak Singh Marg) and three synthetic hornbill feathers adorned the stage. Of the young students around me no one seemed to know what the different colours signified. Although the invitation card to the festival was addressed to 'all members of the Kyong *Community*' (emphasis mine), others were welcome, but there were in fact very few non-northeastern students and faculty. The nicely designed brochure carried images of the male warrior on the left and the woman on the right in traditional costume in static poses, thereby reinforcing the stereotype of 'the tribal', although the intention of these visual icons may have been to trigger off thoughts of the 'heritage'.

Did the festival succeed in suggesting the continuum and the breaks within the community as it were, within generations; did it reflect any of the concerns of the community as a whole? It would be unfair to read too much into a single festival organised by enthusiastic students. The traditional week-long festival had to be compressed to a half a day for obvious reasons. I would argue that for all that it did not or could do, it perfomed one vital function, which was to include people outside the community to at least begin to participate, not as tourists.

The Hornbill Festival (in Delhi) which I attended a few months later took place in Dilli Haat, November 10, 2007. This too had a similar programme: fashion shows, traditional songs sung in choric western harmony (i.e. derived from a very distinctive musical system), as well as some contemporary western songs. The serried ranks of handsome young men and women in traditional attire looking quite comfortable and self-conscious in a proud way, lined up near the entrance to welcome the chief guest.

It is worth noting that the space offered by Delhi Haat is distinct from the usual proscenium stage and auditorium. The Haat, as the name suggests, is a state-sponsored urban site intended to replicate the one-to-one experience of transaction between producer and consumer (without the middle-man, so to speak, the State takes on this role) and offer fair prices to craftspeople from all over the subcontinent on a rotational basis. It would not be too much of an exaggeration to say that this is probably the single most visible place where the average middle-class or upper-class Delhi-ite may have the greatest opportunity for informal interaction with people from different parts of the NE region.

The Haat is laid out in a large vertical rectangle whose inside is contoured with bulges, niches, open air roundabouts, with the wares spilling over, and 'folk artists' singing, dancing or doing puppet shoes. For the most part 'the ethnic' as it is understood in today's advertising language (i.e. as not machine made or imported) is displayed as the still continuing diversity of the nation, packaged not as products but as craftspeople displaying their own work. (This may have been partly inspired from the Craft Museum in Delhi where master craftsmen and women are often invited to work on a residential fellowship of several months.)

In my understanding, the Hornbill Festival at the Dilli Haat was different in the way the participants representing various tribes with weapons of war etc, young men and women, were present in weaving lines, with buyers/spectators almost present as part of the show. This 'breakdown' of the urban proscenium space was refreshing, especially since this did not appear to have been planned.

Similarly, I was struck by the ambivalence of performance '*en costume*': the ease with which one might slip in and out of costume, of displaying and belonging, of 'being' both modern techno-savvy jeans clad youngsters and yet having the possibility of 'representing' ethnic difference to metropolitan audience who are still 'home' i.e. located within the parameters of the constructed urban space offering variety and ware.

However, the tourist brochure which was being distributed in tandem with the performance had a different story to tell. About 'the tourist village' in Mokukchang Dist we are told: 'All the three villages can accommodate considerable tourist[s] in the traditional Naga huts which have *ultra modern facilities with ethnic look*.[40]

The ethnic is thus nudged into a particular shape through the trade routes of tourism, its performance determined in the selective isolation and naming practices of recreating with the intent to offer (for consumption) a privileged glimpse into a 'way of life', slices of 'world-views' that are contained and controlled sometimes with the cooperation and cooptation of its human subjects.

Transnational corporate empires and the supranational flow of goods, peoples and ideas, positing an universal culture have in turn intensified the pressure to produce versions of the local, the ethnic, the regional. The nation-state as well scripts a policy of winning over, of recovery, containing, and displaying its most 'distant' and 'diverse' geo-political part. Thus, container words such as 'heritage' and 'tradition' run the risk of becoming mere bargaining spaces. Our understanding of 'knowledge systems' I would suggest, is being increasingly shaped by the configuration yielded by the two—the global and the local, working not in opposition, but more often than not,[41] working with a common template, that leaves little space for negotiation. I use the word template advisedly. The 'offering' can finally be only an infinite replay, packaged as difference.

The movements into literacy, a written script and westernisation, often through the civilisational ideals of Christianity, and even the adoption of English as an official language bypasses in many ways the by now well-known contradiction of a mainstream *notion* of 'national' culture. At their most radical moments, they may carve out the possibility of exploring untrodden paths. This exploration is vital not only for those most directly involved in these shifts, sometimes condensed within a generation or so, but equally so, for those who would be considered 'outsiders' or who would consider themselves as having already resolved their own tryst with both nation and culture. I would argue in fact that it is precisely those of us who may be situated 'otherwise' who have an obligation to engage with 'knowledge systems' with a fundamental consensus to change.

Among many possibilities that unbounding offers would be an investment in languages, as language itself is the best index of change; it has often functioned as a key site of contestation of identities, albeit with very different allegiances. If one returns then to the word, it can only be as a site of change, even metamorphosis, in which the outsider, the non-native too has to find and earn a space.[42]

[This paper is a revised version of the version presented at the national seminar on 'Literatures and Oratures as Knowledge Systems: Texts from the North-East' CAS, Dept of Comparative Literature, Jadavpur University in January 2009. My sincere thanks to Subha Chakraborty Dasgupta and Samantak Das for provoking me to reflect further on these issues and for their extraordinary patience.]

NOTES

1. For an illuminating exploration, see, R.K.Agnihotri, 'Orality and Literacy in South Asia' in Kachru, B.B. and Sridhar, S.N. ed. *Languages in South Asia*. Cambridge: Cambridge University Press.
2. "Performance and Ethnicity: Towards Contextualising the "Northeast" in India' was presented at the Annual Conference of the International Federation for Theatre Research on 'Ethnicity and Identity Global Performance', Dept of Dramatics, University of Rajasthan and Jawahar Kala Kendra, Jaipur, January 2003, and 'Notes on Two Stories from Manipur' at Indic Religion Conference, New Delhi, December 2003.
3. One of the four districts in Manipur with a concentration of Naga communities.
4. The two stories by Varseo Ningshen were 'Mi Khangayeè: an

ogre-man, but not a man-eating monster' and 'Mahale and the Boa', 2002 (unpublished mss).

5. Indranee Chatterjee, 'Slaves, Souls and Subjects in a South Asian Borderland', p.1.

6. In particular, Chatterjee draws our attention to the 'scripting' of one of the 13 languages into the standardised 'Mizo' language, blurring distinctions of gender, tone and age in the process.

7. 'The name "Manipur" was also coined during his [Garib Niwaz's] reign.'...He took up a series of measures to annihilate the traditional religion [of the Meiteis]'. Sairem Nilabir, 'The Revivalist Movement of Sanamahism' in Naorem Sanajaoba, ed. *Manipur: Past and Present*, Vol. 2, pp. 113-114.

8. 'Lai-Haraoba festival of Manipur deserves to be placed as the most traditional, basic and important festival of the Meiteis, the valley people of Manipur. For a number of reasons, it represents the heart and mind of Meitei culture.' L. Joychandra Singh, 'Matrix of Manipuri Culture: Lai-Haraoba of Manipur'.

9. Jyotindra Jain, Introduction, p. 13.

10. K.S. Singh on dance.

11. Cited in Ramakanta Chakraborty's? *Vaisnavism in Bengal*, 1486-1900, *Introduction to yatras*. Calcutta, Sanskrit Pustak Bhandar, 1985.

12. Muntassir Mamoon, *Unish Shatake Dhakar Theater*.

13. The Brahmo Samaj was established in Dhaka in 1848, but its real impact was felt in the 1860s. Many of the educated professionals such as lawyers, barristers and teachers were enthusiastic about propogating Brahmo ideals. 1860 to 1890 saw an active network of sabhas and samitis, the founding of newspapers and periodicals, including those campaigned for women's education or against child marriage. The weekly *Dhaka Prakash* begun in 1869, had Brahmo editors for the most part. Muntassir Mamoon, *Dhakar Sanskritik Itihaser Upadan*, pp. 72-76.

14. For an overview of the morality debate in the metropolis of Calcutta see my essay "the Second City of the Empire" in *The Indian Economic and Social History Review*, 40, 2, 2003, pp. 192-235.

15. Muntassir Mamoon, *Unish Shatake Dhakar Theater*, p. 10.

16. Muntassir Mamoon, *Unish Shatake Dhakar Theater*, pp. 100-101.
17. Lokendra Arambam, 'The Politics of National Patronage: Shaping a Theatre Modernism for the Periphery: The Manipur Experience', 2008.
18. I have discussed this in some detail in a monograph entitled 'The Dancer and the Dance' (unpublished), a part of which was presented as 'What's dance got to do with it! Morality debates in Bengal, 1920s-1930s and bar-dancers in 21st century India' at an International conference on South Asain Feminisms, Universtity of Pennsylvania, 2008.
19. Pratima Devi, 'Chitrangada Nrityanatya', (BS 1343), p. 27; one of three essays compiled in *Nritya* (Baisakh 1356), Calcutta, Visva-Bharati Publications, rpt. Ashwin 1401.
20. In what was probably one of his most poetical polemics against the concept of the nation, Rabindranath Tagore repeatedly uses the word desh, while taking care to disassociate it from the dominant imagery of the nation as mother.
21. Santidev Ghosh, *Gurudev Rabindranath o Adhunik Bharatiya Nritya*, Baisakh 1390; *Music and Dance in Tagore's Education Philosophy*, 1978.
22. Santidev Ghosh, *Gurudev Rabindranath*, p. 10.
23. Nabakumar came to Santiniketan in 1925-26; and then again in 1934. Santidev Ghosh, *Gurudev Rabindranath*, p. 161
24. Santidev Ghosh, *Gurudev Rabindranath*, pp. 192-93.
25. Santidev Ghosh, *Gurudev Rabindranath*, p. 164.
26. Santidev Ghosh, *Gurudev Rabindranath*, p. 156.
27. Santidev Ghosh, *Music and Dance in Tagore's Education Philosophy*, 54.
28. Santidev Ghosh, *Gurudev Rabindranath*, pp. 30-31.
29. *Desh*, 2nd year, no 15, 2 March 1935, rpt. 17 February 2005, p. 42.
30. Lokendra Aramban, Interview by Biren Das Sharma, *STQ*, 1997, p. 36.

    Macbeth – Stage of Blood was produced first in Ningthen Pukhri in Imphal, June 25, 1997, and subsequently, on the Thames, London.

31. 'Gleanings: Ramkinkar and the other arts' presented at a National Seminar on 'Ramkinkar: Contextualising the Indian Modernist', School of Arts and Aesthetics, Jawaharlal Nehru University, New Delhi, October 29, 2007.

32. The last movement (Urvashi-Pururava encounter) was choreographed in collaboration with Uttara Asha Coorlawala.

33. Chaliah, Debjani. Leija Keioibi (Girl turning into a werewolf) Dance choregraphed with Manipur Dance Academy and performed in Calcutta in 2003.

34. Personal conversation, 20 August 2009.

35. This is a personal and shared reference to a proposal made by some of my M.Phil. students in a workshop on archives that they would like to create a virtual and real archive of 'insurgency'—unpacking the term through image, sound, record, testimony and memory in Manipur and Mizoram. I was moved at their courage and aspiration and immensely saddened at our inability to make such a project possible. The seminar in question was called 'Body in Performance: Comparative Contexts in the 20th Century' and took place in 2009.

36. Jyotindra Jain, p. 00

37. *The North-East Sun*, January 1-14, 2002, vol. 7, no. 1, pp. 8-9.

38. Shailaja Tripathi, 'When the hills sing...' *The Hindu, Metroplus*, Delhi, December 14, 2009.

39. Kalyan Chaudhuri, *Frontline*, January 17, 2003, pp. 68-70.

40. 'Tourist Guide Map of Nagaland (India)', Published by the Ministry of Tourism, Govt of India & Directorate of Tourism, Kohima, Nagaland (not dtd).

41. There are vibrant exceptions of course, as Roma Chatterji tries to show in her article on the contemporary work of traditional scroll painters of Midnapore, Bengal: 'Global Events and Local Narratives: 9/11 and the Picture Storytellers of Bengal'. Department of Sociology, University of Delhi, Occasional Papers (New Series) 2007/4 in *Writing Identities: Folklore and Performative Arts of Purulia*, Bengal (New Delhi, IGNCA, 2009). Chatterji both historicises the cultural region known as 'Purulia' and also seeks to problematise throughout the categories such as the folk and the tribal and their circulation in scholarly discourse. In that the book is cautionary in its tone.

42. Some attempts made in this direction are collaborative projects

with my students which include: 2009 "Sur Pippa: Songs in Many Tongues: Lullabies and Playsongs in Asamiya, Mizo and Kumaoni with translations into English' (publication forthcoming). Introduction by Rimli Bhattacharya. Project members: Prachee Dewri, Kristina Zama, Padmakshi Patowary and Aditi Chand.2009 A study of 'Subject English' in NCERT textbooks (Classes 3-5), including classroom observation and alternative pedagogies (publication forthcoming). Introduction by Rimli Bhattacharya. Nivedita Basu, Anuja Madan, Sreyoshi Sarkar. In this project Anuja Madan has also looked at the actual classroom transaction of a story from Manipur, 'Who will be Ningthou?'.

Both projects have a team of 3-4 researchers, most of whom are former MPhil students. The projects have been supported by Eklavya and the Ratan Tata Trust.

REFERENCES

Arambam, Lokendra. 'The Politics of National Patronage: Shaping a Theatre Modernism for the Periphery: The Manipur Experience.' Paper presented at Seminar on Reviewing Disciplinary Agendas in Theatre Studies: Cultural Arenas, Policies, Institutions, IEG, New Delhi, 2008.

Bharucha, Rustom. *The Theatre of Kanhailal, Pebet and Memoirs of Africa*, Calcutta, Seagull Books, 1992.

Ghose, Santidev. *Gurudeb Rabindranath o Adhunik Bharatiya Nritya* ((BS 1390) (Gurudev Rabindranath and Modern Indian Dance). Calcutta, Ananda Publishers, Baisakh, 1414 rpt.

Ghose, Santidev. *Music and Dance in Rabindranath Tagore's Education [sic] Philosophy*. New Delhi: Sangeet Natak Akademi, 1978.

Lonsdale, John. 'Globalization, Ethnicity and Democracy: A View from the "Hopeless Continent"', pp. 194-219.

Jain, Jyotindra, Introduction. Image mobility in India's popular culture. *Marg*, 2007, pp. 7-17.

Jain, Jyotindra, 'India's Republic Day Parade', Image mobility in India's popular culture. *Marg*, 2007, pp. 62-75.

Mamoon, Muntassir. *Unish Shatake Dhakar Theater* (Theatre in 19th Century Dhaka). Dhaka: 1979.

Mamoon, Muntassir. *Dhakar Sanskritik Itihaser Upadan*. Dhaka, Pallab Publishers, 1999.

Miri, Mrinal. ed. *Continuity and Change in Tribal Society*, Shimla, Indian Institute of Advanced Studies, 1993.

Singh, K.S. 'Tribal Perspectives—1969-1990' in Miri, Mrinal ed. *Continuity and Change in Tribal Society*. Shimla, Indian Institute of Advanced Studies, 1993, pp. 5-10.

Sanajaoba, Naorem. *Manipur: Past and Present*, Volume 2. New Delhi, Mittal Publications, 1991.

Sinha, C. 'Christianity and Ethnic Identity Among the Nagas' in Miri, Mrinal. ed. *Continuity and Change in Tribal Society*, Shimla, Indian Institute of Advanced Studies, 1993, pp. 142-57.

8

'Exotica' or Ethics? Reviewing the Aesthetics and Politics of Contemporary Manipuri Theatre

Epsita Halder

In the play *Chakravyuha,* directed by Ratan Thiyam of Manipur, when Abhimanyu fights simultaneously with stalwarts like Duryodhana, Jayadratha, Shalya and Aswathama in the *Chakravyuha*, the gestured cues that create the meaning of the bodily engagements between the hero and his enemy are addressed to an initiated audience. The audience can understand the figures and figurations as belonging to a culture of bodies and rituals that sanctify the bodily performances. It can easily be inferred that the physical movements of the warriors were not improvised to create a massive spatial tension; rather they followed a specific form; to be more specific, a stylized dance-form. This is called Thang-Ta, "the art of sword and spear". Initially used in warfare, the extended ritualistic domain of sacrifice and immolation, it was prohibited by the British colonizers between 1891 and 1947. When Thiyam uses this form on stage to create a kinesthetic action-interaction of the actors, it fulfills two purposes. Through the practice of Thang-Ta, a phenomenological consciousness is created in terms of the interaction between the actors and a responsive audience. In the structure of the retention and release of bodily energy, a total coordination of collective body parts is achieved by which one actor's body responds to another's in terms of bodily reflex.[1] Secondly, used and explored as a dramatic technique, this particular martial expression of the indigenous Manipuri community produces the *rasa* of the situation. Later on, we will see that Heisnam Kanhailal, another contemporary director of Manipur, would also adapt this martial form as a kinetic-spiritual exercise to train the body of the actor[2].

Now, my question is: what is the significance of the adaptation of this form? Is it only an apparatus to achieve phenomenological goals, making the body a structured repository of knowledge without much cerebral interpretive engagement with the dramatic situation? Or is this a formative tool of a region to actualize the Rasa system? Region means location. When it is a regional indigenous system of expressions, is the standardized Sanskritized Rasa system rearticulated and relocated in terms of the region and its relationship with the "standard-national"? Alternatively, does it remain a purely formal tool? When the body is invoked both as a source and disseminator of knowledge, there is a philosophy and aesthetics of the body. But my question is whether it is a political motivation, a demand of the everyday social experience, involved in the conceptualization of that philosophy and that aesthetics of that body?

I will limit this paper to the discussion of the theatre of Ratan Thiyam and Kanhailal, the two most visible icons of contemporary Manipuri theatre. My discussion will be on the particular theatrical embodiment of the actor's body which defines the form of the play. However, it will also be a discussion on the tension between the demands of the form and the demands of the content that creates the viability of a regional theatrical expression. While discussing form, we will be able to touch upon a variety of indigenous expressions starting from Thang-Ta to Chola-Cholum as physical expressions, and content ranging from the adaptation of the Sanskrit epic to Manipuri folktales.

The specific historico-political location of Manipur in the context of the forces of the nation-state and the official agendas of the post-independence Indian theatre needs to be addressed to understand Manipuri theatre as a regional expression.

Manipur is a state where the Meitei, or the majority indigenous community, live in the central trough-like valley, and 32 Naga and Kuki communities live in the hills. The Meitei community converted to Vaishnavism with the advent of the mainland Vaishnava cult in the 18th century. Indigenous Meitei holy books called *puya* were burnt in a violent suppression of the resisting locals. Stability finally arrived with the Vaishnava royal power standardizing and popularizing performative forms like *Rasa Lila* and *Natasangkirtana,* which socio-politically consolidated a new Vaishnava Manipur[3]. In the hegemonic process of Hinduization in Manipur, Meitei gods were replaced by the Vedic pantheon where Pakhangba became Shiva, Panthoibi became Durga and Thungjing became Vishnu. Under the violent British rule during Warren Hastings's time, the state's name was changed from Sannaleipak, land of goddess Sannamahi, to a Sanskritized Manipur. The period between 1890 and 1930 was the high noon of other forces like Christianization and expansion of English education. Simultaneously, the Bangla script reached Manipur as the official graphic expression of the Meitei language. A Manipuri literary modernism started developing, led by the Sanskrit, Bengali and Hindu models.

The British ruled Manipur, which was a protected kingdom until 1947, and which experienced diverse anti-British movements like the First Women's Agitation of 1904, the Kuki Rebellion of 1917-19, the Zeliangrong Movement of 1930-32, the Water Tax Movement and the Women's Agitation of 1939. In 1949, Manipur was converted to a 'Part C' state from an independent one by merging it with Shillong, Assam. After a long bloody journey of protest which the Indian Government termed 'insurgence', Manipur was finally granted statehood in 1972, but the draconian Armed Forces Special Powers Act of 1958 which gave the Indian Army massive powers to arrest and 'interrogate' any so-called 'suspect' has not yet been withdrawn. So what we have here is a very complex network of political tensions between the centre and the state, the national and the regional beneath the umbrella of 'Indian democracy'. What is clearly articulated is the lack of communication between national and regional cultures, an incommensurability that is cultivated to perpetuate a solid centre-margin relationship, a Hindu-ethnic divide. This lacuna of communication is symptomatic of the way the nation-state conceptualized its history—separated from its primitive other, the other-within. The othering of the ethnic was a process to discover/rediscover and define/redefine the 'primitive-within' by relegating it to the purity of the corporeal[4]. History, as a rational textualization of the events in real time and real space, created the ethnic as non-historical (as having a non-viable consciousness of the relationship between time and space). Through the simultaneous inauguration of history and ethnology as disciplines, the historical subject became the rational/national subject by a process of dissociating 'his' history from that of the 'primitive'.

In colonial Bengal, a very interesting dynamics between history and anthropology was found which would echo the Fabian concept that the sense of historical time in the West was founded on the anthropological invention of 'people without history'[5]. The post-independence period was Nehruvian in its attempt to redefine the national by addressing the regional cultures as creating viable national identities. In the assimilative forces of the national institutions, a diverse cultural heritage was brought in to give rise to a 'common' national expression, political solidarity and belongingness was sought in terms of cultural cohesion through a populist slogan 'Unity in Diversity'. Following the Third Five Year Plan, "the success of economic planning in India will largely depend upon our capacity to hold together as a nation in the midst of diversity of language, region, caste and religion"[6], unity in a democracy "must be based on the consciousness of a common cultural heritage"[7]. Under the project of decolonization, an indigenous/regional aesthetics of performance was reclaimed to realize a heterogeneous space called postcolonial India and collective articulation as Indian cultural heritage. This language of difference and sameness was articulated in the fields of literature, theatre and other cultural expressions like visual arts through institutionalized government bodies like the Sahitya Academy, the Sangeet Natak Academy and the Lalit Kala Academy. In this context, traditional Indian performances were considered to be a move away from the text-based proscenium-oriented naturalism to achieve performative decolonization and a re-assertion of Indian-ness.

Modern Indian theatre's 'encounter with tradition' was considered to be functional for the 'liberation from Western realistic theatre.'[8] In the post-Independence period, classical dances, rituals, martial arts and popular entertainment were identified as traditionally Indian. Seen through the lens of Sanskrit aesthetic theory, a different kind of dramaturgical structure, acting style and staging technique emerged to create a distinct and separate meaning of the classical vis-à-vis the regional/folk/indigenous.[9]

While Dr. Awasthi's theorization re-enacted the Orientalist binary and colonial rationality where he valorized 'indigenous' theatre, the movement of the roots actually helped create a different notion of the performance text. But leaving Dr. Awasthi aside, theoreticians also defined it as a "quest ... not so much for a 'national theatre' as for a significance theatre in and of the nation, linked intra-nationally by complex commonalities and mutual self-differentiations."[10] This was the radical moment in Indian theatre because by incorporating indigenous folk expressions from ritualistic configurations to everyday modes of enunciation, it physicalized the text and the stage. Starting from the training sessions of the actors to audience perception, it invoked a complete different set of sensibility, prompting 'a culture-specific and site-based reading'[11] of modernity. So, when any Manipuri theatre personality involves a series of indigenous materials as tools of physicalization and generic expression, we need to focus on whether this indigeneity creates an interpretive framework as well. By re-articulating the question already raised in the very beginning of this article, we can lay the groundwork of a more focussed problematic: are indigenous expressions, in terms of both form and content, when adapted by the dramatist-director, re-contextualized to serve a specific purpose of modernity? How can the process of adapting a certain form be interpreted? Is it determined out of the demand of the content or is it an interpretation of the content itself? Or is it a formal move to utilise the indigenous/folk form into something new?

To start with Ratan Thiyam who initiated the journey of his group, The Chorus Theatre Repertory, one cannot escape from his *Mahabharata* trilogy, *Urubhangam*, *Chakravyuha* and *Karnabharam*. It is very interesting to note that the first and the last plays were an adaptation of the Bhasa plays with the same names. KN Panikkar also staged *Urubhangam* in 1987 using the Kathakali repertoire as an expression of *thanathunatakavedi* (literally "our own theatre"). Ratan Thiyam shared Panikkar's ideology of combining the regional dramaturgical structure and methods of physical training with the aesthetic theory of the *Natyasastra*. The aesthetic goal that Thiyam wanted to reach was based on readings of Sanskrit aesthetics which he executed through the indigenous realisation of the self and embodiment of regional subjectivity. Now the question remains: how can this re-contextualization be read as the politics of performance that can be instrumental in understanding the language of modernism in Manipur?

In the opening scene of *Karnabharam*, the Nandi breaks into *Natasangkirtana* steps and energizes the space in such a way that the rigid parameters of the proscenium relax, giving rise to a sense of the *mandapa*, as an open arena for both the secular and ritualistic spaces. The slow and lyrical body language of *Natasangkirtana* in the next phase transforms into a sharper, more rapid and martial one, establishing the ambience of the play's heroic thematic. This shift in the body language creates a hybrid space (between indigenous and high Hindu Vaishnavism) so symptomatic and emblematic of the Manipuri culture. The performance is punctuated with the presence of the narrator and the drummers. The drummers performing the traditional acrobatic Pung-Cholam dance destabilize the division between the sacred arena and the performative/theatrical arena. The transformation of dance steps from lyrical to martial is an engagement with the Meitei past where Meitei is conceptualized as a hybrid cultural space, hybridity being the historical consciousness of Manipur. It can retain ethnic martial dance steps simultaneously with its newfound faith in the Krishna cult. But is it interpreted similarly to contextualize the choice of different formal aesthetic devices together, or is it a pure exercise of form or technique?

In an interview taken in 2005 for a documentary series on

contemporary Indian theatre directors (directed by Somnath Gupta), Ratan Thiyam said that form is dictated by the content and music, narrative style. Everything else evolves accordingly. If that is so, then, what is the uniqueness in the content, the driving force behind the narratorial and formative decisions that Ratan Thiyam chooses to express his message? In his *Mahabharata* trilogy, Ratan Thiyam takes an intimate look at the classical anti-heroes and non-heroes like Karna and Abhimanyu to destabilize the celebrated notion of heroism and refute the rationale of war and violence. But what is the justification of commenting upon the same universal values with region-specific formal devices of the Meitei, if the content of the plays cannot be instruments to engage with the political situation of Manipur? This has been one constant allegation against Ratan Thiyam by Manipur's intelligentsia, despite his overarching popularity, both national and international.

Ratan Thiyam offered a space of reception in adapting Manipuri indigenous forms to tell stories from the *Mahabharata*. The status of the *Mahabharata*, like that of the *Ramayana*, cannot be understood as a single and fixed text, but as a multi-vocal entity, a polyphony of (in)versions encompassing various retellings which emerged out of different regions through formal and ideological negotiations. Sheldon Pollock commented on these retellings of the epic tradition as varying 'according to historical period, regional literary tradition, religious affiliation, genre, and political context'[12]. Then, does the story of Manipur reside in the generalized *shoka* produced out of the death of the anti-hero Duryodhana? Or does Abhimanyu represent the situation of the Manipuri youth, who are lulled to war for the so-called greater common good of the state, or is he Manipur herself, who has lost her valid weapon to the more powerful enemy, the central government or the army, to fight a battle to acquire her own legitimacy? In the dynamics of postcolonial India's history, is not Manipur produced as Abhimanyu who doesn't have the access to complete knowledge/power and isn't this carefully constructed inaccessibility the cause of Manipur's political trauma? So the epic tradition must be a textual space where different locations of utterance can actualize themselves in different historical conjunctures. Here, Thiyam used the narrator from the traditional Wari-Leeba performance. Through Wari-Leeba, the indigenous form for epic performance, a common cultural heritage was formed in Manipur. It is because of this tradition that the mighty larger-than-life epic protagonists are considered relatable to everyday mundane human beings.

Wari-Leeba, using minimal gestures, explores speech and vocal power as two basic elements of communication, both material and medium. Voice has been used to communicate the denotative and connotative use of the words in a way that breaks down the division between the matter and the means, between content and form. Thus, bringing in this tradition, Ratan Thiyam proposes and successfully recreates the ideologies of the oral performance. Thiyam said that Wari-leeba 'paints pictures through words'[13]; his critics have also celebrated the pure formal possibility of this adaptation. Ratan Thiyam overemphasized the 'select[ion] not the words, but the modes of delivery, the tonal quality'[14] to intensify the thematic arrangements of the dramatic situations. Though it should be acknowledged that it is this treatment of vocality that produces a language in itself, a very strong and important theatrical device, 'the true language of the piece is visceral and absolutely clear'[15], and this way 'Thiyam has done nothing less than go beyond language altogether.'[16] Here, we see a particular consideration and theorization, which proposes vocal expression, irrespective of it being non-discursive, in a specific condition, embodiment and form of language, thus establishing the ethics of orality as an integral part of Manipuri literary and performative modernism. Then we can also presume that Ratan Thiyam has almost answered his own question: 'How can an actor create a language of expression?'[17]

Here, following the description of expressive forms as quadralogue[18] I would like to invite a necessary reading of the various receptions of Ratan Thiyam's aesthetics of production. It will be an interesting errand to focus on the location of critical utterances. It is at the international arena that this de-contextualized theory of language evolved, where the form was understood as a pure vehicle of thought, sometimes a thought-in-itself, to reciprocate and communicate a particular kind of theme: a retelling of an epic.

In *Chakravyuha*, in the *Nandi* section, a flag is offered during worship or puja while the narrator chants mantras for different Vedic deities. A particular indigenous form of the flag has been used in the Nandi section, which remains throughout the play as an inescapable prop, tempting us to read the presence of this omnipresent sign. So, when the narrator speaks in the prologue section, "National flags conceptualize politics. In this modern battlefield, the holy plains of Kurukshetra, the power game has already started. This is a war of flags...this is a war of power gabblers"[19], it signifies a conscious shift from the epic vocabulary creating a space for interpretation. But what is the interpretation? Ratan Thiyam constantly talks about the Third World and global power in the context of his drama, elaborating on notions like war and peace. When he uses the narrator to comment on the universal game of politics using the format of the traditional *Mahabharata* performance, we grow curiously restless at the absence of any specific Manipuri content in that comment. Neither has any kind of defamatory tactic been deployed the way it was done by Mahasweta Devi in *Dauloti* nor is any propagandist retelling of the *Mahabharata* expected. But Thiyam is using a traditional poetic strategy of Wari-Leeba to distance the narrator from the course of the narrative, to comment on it while standing at a completely different timeframe at a different chronotope. The moment of dissociation in terms of time and space offers an open end inside the narrative, where a subtext could be proposed and built to connect the timeless universality of the epic message with the particularity of the present. We can assume that here, in *Chkravyuha*, Ratan Thiyam had enormous scope to politicize the indigenous narrative tradition of Wari-Leeba as well. What he did with traditional performative expression was for the sake of satisfying a pure aesthetic purpose. Politicization of the content by contextualizing it within contemporary Centre-Manipur tensions would have inevitably politicized the use of the indigenous form, surely carving out a political performative agenda that can only be located in the Manipuri socio-cultural experience.

If we look at the responses from Imphal, we will see that Ratan Thiyam is having a hard time satisfying his discerning audience within Manipur. Premchand Nongthombam, theatre director and critic, did not mince words when he said that *Chakravyuha* was not "meaningful or relevant to the reality that Ratan Thiyam himself was facing here in Manipur".[20] SK Mangang, Director of Marjingkhol Cultural-cum-Drama Association, expressed similar sentiments about *Chakravyuha*, saying that it did not "represent the tensions of the reality he is living in".[21] Premchand sounded quite harsh in critiquing the relationship between its theme, form and the international funding agency that patronized that kind of Manipuri theatre, "We have learnt to look at our realities, at our own tradition, with the outlook of our promoters who are from different cultural and political contexts".[22] Lokendra Arambam was rhetorical yet direct: "Ratan Thiyam initially transcended local and regional frontiers to seek greener pastures."[23] Ratan Thiyam did move away from the much-criticized position that he held earlier, but that needs to be understood not only as an outcome of the dialogue between the director and the critic, but also as a result of his reception of other contemporary theatre aesthetics.

Before referring to the processes of reception, we need to study the use of theatrical devices and thematic choices made by H Kanhailal, the other important face of Manipuri theatre. I realize it is quite impossible to talk about contemporary Manipuri theatre without referring to Premchand and Arambam. (The latter is a documentary filmmaker as well, which gives him, and through him, us, a different analytical eye to look at Manipuri theatre.[24]) By limiting myself to the study of Kanhailal's production I will say that Kanhailal, back in the mid-1970s, had already established himself as a political thinker through his group Kalakshetra, by directing *Imphal 1973* and *Pebet*. His encounter with Badal Sircar in the 1970s and the ideology of the Third Theatre inspired and prompted him to evolve a theatrical language with a non-verbal idiom. *Pebet*, the story of a bird-mother and her children and their encounter with a seductive cat who plans to 'eat' the children, is a modern stylized adaptation of a Manipuri folktale. *Pebet* has been projected and read as a critique of the Hinduization of the ethnic community, namely the Meitei.

While watching Kanhailal's plays and analysing them, we cannot escape the presence of the central woman figure in each and every play—*Imphal 1973, Pebet, Dakghar, Draupadi* and the *Memoirs of Africa*. She is Sabitri Heisnam. While performing in *Memoirs of Africa*, a Kanhailal production based on a poem of the same name composed by L Samarendra Singh, her body becomes the embodiment of universal suffering and sorrow. The physicality of pain and corporeal violence was being enacted through the materiality of this elderly actor's body. It was a story of the eternal persecution and survival of Mi, a person who could be either man or woman, played by Sabitri who used the dual images of a tree and a slave to evoke the sheer magnitude of struggle. She is accompanied by two Nupis played by two young women in traditional Rasa Lila attire. Kanhailal justified his doing *Memoirs of Africa* in an interview with Rustom Bharucha, "People, whether they are Naga or Meitei or African, cannot ultimately be suppressed".[25] Bharucha seemed a bit annoyed at the universalist tone prevalent in Kanhailal's interpretation of violence and suffering in the production. Mi, the innocent natural force, is constantly transformed into the eternal figures of peasant or slave or everything that can be subjugated brutally. Yet, this is neither a direct nor a suggestive portrayal of Manipur. But when a universal theme and a specific formal local language of enunciation connect, we should focus on the specificity of the embodiment of bodily and psychic experiences to see whether the production really remains universalist.

As a performance-production, it has very few intelligible words, other than just one song, 'hoi' being the only intelligible word with which Sabitri, Mi, calls the Nupis who come to play with her at the moment of fertile abundance and happiness. Only a suggestive extra-literary sound pattern has been used to create the mood of the situation, like "he ui iiii iiii/ he ui i i i i i i i i/ he ee u iii ii i" and during the perpetration of violence, almost as a shout, "SHET SHET SHET SHET". The moment of bliss is expressed through song or silence prevailing around the gestures and calm facial expressions of Sabitri/Mi. Neither do we get to know the names of the characters nor are we able to locate them in the folkloric tradition of Manipur as we are denied any narrative cue. What we see visually and experience physically is through the presence of Sabitri and her co-actors, through the aesthetic-phenomenological mediation of the performing figures. The director, as was revealed in the interview, wanted to give us an experience of not only trans-border suffering but also a trans-gendered one, which exceeds the gendered binary by disclosing the violation of a tree or of nature as a whole through the performer's body. A very strange situation transpires on stage when the apparent biological markers of gender of the actors replicate the language of gendered violence. Though a woman actor was enacting/personifying the trauma of nature when she/it was whipped brutally by the men surrounding her/it, she/it did not fully actualize the gendered Sabitri as the defined materiality of her body. The trans-border is associated with the trans-gendered experience which also includes the neuter. But what happened on stage while expressing the sufferings of/in Africa is that Kanhailal relocated the codes of Manipuri ritualistic body-aesthetics in a new context of the body: Sabitri's body wearing an everyday black *phanek* and blouse is placed outside the ritualistic context. When Sabitri was dancing and gesticulating otherwise it was not a pure connection with the pure form with all its extravagant attire and accessories like those of the Thiyam plays, but a processed form, received, interpreted and re-enacted by the character(s). The dichotomy between Sabitri and the Nupis — Sabitri dressed in black and the elaborately dressed Nupis doing a Rasa Lila proper — and their dual onstage presence produce a third level of meaning, of deviation from the blissful organic spiritual-aesthetic wholeness. Nupis, as playmates of Mi, lament over her/his/its suffering or Africa's suffering, but the immediate visual implication of a particular body kinesthetic (both ritualistic and an improvised heightened ordinary) unknowingly channelizes us towards the embodiment of Manipur herself. No matter how much Kanhailal may talk about universalism, the presence of Manipur in terms of the Nupis' attire and ritualistic body language and its lack in Sabitri's created a nuanced interaction between the ritual and the performance, between the sacred and the profane, producing an interpretive framework within the performance text itself.

Manipur may not be the essence of the performance, but it showed a space of negotiation between the aesthetics and the contemporary realities of Manipur. Theoretically, it was explained in the brochure that oppressive power which was symbolized and performed by three male figures, was the enactment of the Second World War. But on stage, a feminine figure surrounded by three male figures with bare torsos with high boots and leather-strapped trousers invoke a very specific context of the gendered experience of Manipur. At moments when the embodiments of gendered violence got solidified on stage, it invoked what Kanhailal may not or did not intend to invoke.

This production was followed by his stage adaptation of 'Draupadi', (a short story by Mahasweta Devi) in 2000. The lead female role of Dopdi Mejhen was again played by Sabitri. Dopdi, hailing from an ethnic community, was involved in an underground Naxalite movement, and when caught, was gang-raped by the army. The short story's stunning climax shows Dopdi stripping off her clothes, violently angry, to face the General, defiance and anger writ large on her raped and wounded body. Here, she carried the imprint/language of resistance on her body, where her violated and traumatized feminine body is not a site of victimhood, but a repository of public anger and protest. In the 2000 play, the defiant self-stripped body of Dopdi/Sabitri symbolized the condition of the women of Manipur, creating a tremendous emotional impact on the minds of the audience after the media highlighted the ongoing political turmoil of Manipur. In July 2004, a group of Manipuri women — middle-aged mothers — stripped themselves naked in front of Kangla Fort, the headquarters of the Indian Army in Imphal, holding a banner that read "Indian Army Rape Us" to protest the alleged abduction, gang-rape and murder of Thangjam Manorama (a 32-year old woman) by the Indian Army and demanded that the Armed Forces Special Powers Act of 1958 be repealed.[26] The female body thus becomes, in reality, the site for the declaration of war, a specific war that cannot be subsumed in any epic formation without deviating from it. The women will have to be Dopdis, rather than the epic Draupadi, though the thematic is age-old. It is also the story of Manipuri mothers who are both community healers and perpetrators of violence. It is interesting to note that the presence of Sabitri Devi as a moving force in the evolution of the theatrical language of Kalakshetra generated the gendered experience in a more complicated manner, going beyond the material fixity of gender.

Here, the presence of Sabitri Devi is hauntingly significant. We can assume that both the form and the content of the plays are related to her enormous theatrical talent and expertise in traditional dance forms and martial arts. Starting from *Imphal 1973* to *Draupadi*, Sabitri's presence and enactment reinforce both a feminine/mother figure (that has been the pivot of almost all plays except *Dakghar*) and a destabilization of the fixed materiality of that gendered-generational existence. She played Amol in their latest production of Tagore's *Dakghar*, which inaugurated a different kind of experience—of alienation and the pain and intensity of a futile waiting. Amol, a seven-year-old boy in the text, transcended the materiality of gender and age when he was embodied by Sabitri Devi on stage. Throughout the performance Sabitri Devi enclosed and restricted her movements within a small circle downstage. When other characters entered the stage, they used the upstage. There was a non-returning of gaze between Amol and other characters as Amol/Sabitri Devi fixed her face towards the audience using improvised Rasa Lila steps, hence finally a non-connection between the self and the other, the interior and the exterior, between man and nature, between desire and its fulfillment, was achieved. Rasa Lila steps were made profane by using them outside the domain of ritual proper, in the realm of the trivial and everyday. On the one hand, that expands the scope of the interpretive framework, universalizing the textual particularity, and on the other, that particularized the abstract experience of alienation by contextualizing it. This context is Manipur itself.

A highly structured aesthetic schema of Ratan Thiyam which includes both the ethnic and the Vaishnavite cultural expressions shows that there can be no exclusivity for both the expressions. He presents Manipur as a historically hybrid moment. But the absence of the profane or at least a profane framework around these highly ritualized/standardized kino-aesthetics makes a space for pure aesthetic language which connects the high Sanskrit with the poetics of the local. As two aesthetic schools are made to meet deliberately and enter into dialogue with each other, an aesthetic hybridity is produced which gets politically charged. By the political I do not intend to mean that Manipuri theatre should adopt a socialist realist position to textualize her uniquely brutalized marginality in a post-independent India.

Do we have any problem in reading it as 'Memoirs of Manipur'? Can we fail to notice a volcanic eruption of anger emerging from the brutalized feminine body? I am tempted to say 'from the mother's body' considering her age and the kind of emotive relation Sabitri forges between her and her audience through her elderly body. I should also say that she performs with such raw emotion, sometimes so childlike, that at times she transcends her literal age. Let us look at the embodiment and processing of emotion in this sequence by Sabitri. Ratan Thiyam said in an interview that ritualistic processions and other expressions on stage are not rituals as they are used as formal devices to evolve the Rasa; repeatedly, his characters talk about the primacy of Sanskrit aesthetics while his actors relocate Rasa in the local aesthetic idioms like the Wari-Leeba tradition. But at Kalakhsetra, through the trance-like emotive-physical exercise, a de-location of the Rasa theory and then a re-location of it are achieved. The use of the shamanic ritualistic embodiment of trance contextualizes ritualistic processes to fit a contemporary purpose, to evolve a modern language for Manipuri theatre. The conception of this figure as a liminal gendered being between the sacred and the profane, between ritual and theatre/everyday, are interesting tipping points of the language of Manipuri theatre, but obviously I am not going into those details.

Finally, let's end with Ratan Thiyam. This study will remain incomplete if I don't refer to Thiyam's recent productions like *Imphal Imphal* and *Nine Hills One Valley* which use a more direct political language, proving that one's formal exercise in aesthetics cannot remain in a purely aesthetic domain when political unrest looms large in the lives of one's people as a life-threatening reality.

NOTES & REFERENCES

1. Thiyam, Ratan Thiyam, *Chakravyuha, pretext and performance text* by Kavita Nagpal, Seagull Books, 1998.

2. Bharucha, Rustam, *The Theatre of Kanhailala: Pebet and Memoirs of Africa*, Seagull Books, Kolkata, 1992.

3. Arambam, Lokendra, 'Manipuri Theatre', in Ananda Lal (ed) *The Oxford Companion to Indian Theatre*, OUP, New Delhi, 2004, pp. 251-253.

4. Banerjee, Prathama, *Politics of Time: 'Primitives' and History-writing in a Colonial Society*, OUP, New Delhi, 2006.

5. *Ibid.*, p. 25.

6. The Third Five Year Plan, Delhi, Government of India, 1961, p. 317.

7. *Ibid.*

8. Awasthi, Dr Suresh, "Theatre of Roots": Encounter with Tradition', *TDR*, 33(4), 1989, p. 48. Dr Suresh Awasthi was among the most important theoreticians of this movement – the theatre of the roots. This movement preferred a committed renewal of the folk performances to create a modern Indian theatrical tradition. Though the attempt in terms of practice was not unilinear, one can easily name K.N. Panikkar, Shanta Gandhi, Vijay Tendulkar, Habib Tanvir among the pioneers of this movement.

9. Mee, Erin B, *Theatre of Roots: Redirecting the Modern Indian Stage*, Seagull, Calcutta, 2007, p. 5.

10. Dharwadker, *Theatres of Independence: Drama, Theory, and Urban Performance in India since 1947*, University of Iowa Press, Iowa City, 2005, p. 24.

11. Gaonkar, Dilip, 'On Alternative Modernities', in Dilip Parameswar Gaonkar (ed), *Alternative Modernities*, Duke University Press, Durham, 2001, p. 14.

12. Pollock, Sheldon, 'Ramayana and Political Imagination of India', *Journal of Asian Studies*, vol. 52, no.2, May 1993, p. 263.

13. Jacob, Paul (ed), *Contemporary Indian Theatre: Interviews with Playwrights and Directors*, Sangeet Natak Academy, 1989a, p. 140.

14. Kothari, Sunil, 'The Man from Manipur', as referred in Erin Mee, *ibid*, p. 258.

15. Drostova, Lisa, 'Redemption and Thrills', *East Bay Express*, 13 October, 2000, as referred in Mee, ibid, p. 259.

16. Thayil, Jeet, *Uttar-Priyadarshi: Thiyam's Manipuri War-Play, India Abroad*, 27 October, 2000, as referred in Mee, *ibid*, p. 259.

17. Mee, *ibid*, p.259, interview taken by the author, 2000, New York.

18. According to Sutton Smith, "If language is always dialogue, a situated act, and not merely a text, that all expressive forms, of which play is only one, are a quadralogue. They always involve at least four prototypical parts." Actors and co-actors, audience, director and the critic/commentator. As quoted in Richard Schechner and Willa Appel (eds), *By Means of Performance: Intercultural Studies of Theatre*, Cambridge University Press, Cambridge, 1990, p. 6.

19. Thiyam, Ratan, *Chakravyuha: Pretext and Performance Text* (ed) Kavita Nagpal, Seagull Books, 1998, p. 10.

20. In Katyal, Anjum and Naveen Kishore, '"Still Searching": A Panel Discussion with Directors of the Nineties', Seagull Theatre Quarterly, 14/15:117-137, 1997

21. *Ibid.*, p. 23.

22. Premchand, Nongthombam, 'One Hundred Years of Colonial Theatre and Resistance to It', in L Damodar Singh, Lokendra Arambam and Nongthombam Premchand (eds), *100 Years of Manipuri Proscenium Arch Theatre*, Department of Arts and Culture, Government of Manipur, 2002, p. 23.

23. Arambam, *ibid.*, p. 253.

24. Arambam's documentary and Kanhailal's *Droupadi* were clubbed together for screening and performance, respectively, at the 2005 Nandikar Theatre Festival at Kolkata. These two modes of re-presentation create a combined space articulating the necessity of certain forms to portray a contemporary Manipur. Arambam's hard-hitting documentary format to depict the violent oppression of the Armed Special Power Force on Manipuri men and women and Heisnam's staging of a slice of the Naxalite movement where a woman tribal activist named Dopdi Mejhen would be raped in custody, connect the language of political reality with the language of aesthetics.

25. Bharucha, 'Politics of Indigenous Theatre: Konhailal of Manipur', *Economic and Political Weekly*, Vol. 26, No. 11/12. Annual Number (March 1991, p. 799.

26. *The Telegraph*, 25 July, 2004.

9

"The Trickster Figure" in North-Eastern Folklore: Contemporary Transformations in an Ao Naga Short Story

Debashree Dattaray

The word itself, 'research' is probably one of the dirtiest words in the Indigenous world's vocabulary. When mentioned in many Indigenous contexts, it stirs up silence, it conjures up bad memories, it raises a smile that is knowing and distrustful.[1]

Embarking upon a journey of reading north-eastern folklore, I am cautioned by the words of Maori writer Linda Tuhiwai Smith. "Indigenity" itself is defined as the quality of being 'born in a region' [OED], which is considered as "otherness" based on "preconceived notions of Native cultures and peoples as "static" and on mystifications of a land-based ideology."[2] Therefore, as a 'researcher' in folk literatures in northeast India, I am apprehensive of being only a cog in the wheel that accentuates the concept of 'Other' through "institutions, vocabulary, scholarship, imagery, doctrines, even colonial bureaucracies and colonial styles".[3] Moreover, a certain degree of cautiousness is attached to the word 'north-eastern' itself. On the one hand, it indicates a geographical space on the north-eastern part of India. On the other hand, the ambivalence of the term introduces one to the different levels of 'otherness'. It epitomizes years of struggle against the imperialistic motivations of neighbouring states, and by extension, a tendency to homogenize all as 'north-eastern'. Given the multiplicity of communities amongst the 'seven sisters' in the north-eastern parts of India, it is definitely presumptuous to consider all cultural attributes under an umbrella term such as 'north-eastern'. In recent years, scholars, and activists have articulated a response against the homogenized, monolithic concept of the "north-eastern" by way of anthologies, monographs, and recordings. While there are points of commonality between all cultures, stories from each culture reflect life-worlds based in a particular region, socially and geographically.

At this point, one may ask as to how one gauges the particularities of a community from an outsider's point of view, and what should be a valid standpoint for a discussion on the same. It is, perhaps, only possible to forge connections by being sensitive to specific historical and discursive practices which in turn, would involve a different construction in reading practices. The alternative therefore is to allow a reading from below. This would mean that the literary work would dictate the modes of analysis, and these modes would enable the construction of specific theoretical formulations. Advocated by Indian comparatist, Amiya Dev, "Comparative Literature from below" propounds a centrifugal approach to literary investigation. In such a case, the literary work is not doctored to suit any particular theoretical or ideological assumptions. This is probably one of the basic and essential differences between the fast emerging Culture Studies in the west, and the methodology practiced within the purview of comparative literature in India. A sensitive engagement with northeastern folk literatures in India is possible only within the context of Comparative Literature methodology "from below". Reflected in the acceptance of "all varieties of texts as legitimate semiotic areas"[4] at any given point of time, there exists "the possibility of interpenetration of these areas or of a variety of semiotic behavior"[5] on the part of the reader.

As I try to harp on my 'cultural sensitivity' and reservations of treading an unsure, academic path, I am also aware of the "cultural difference approach" which reinforces an important epistemological cornerstone of imperialism: the colonized possess a series of knowable characteristics and can be studied, known, and managed accordingly by the colonizers whose own complicity remains unmasked.[6]

Location as I would be elaborating may not necessarily justify the vantage point as a researcher in folk literatures but it might help cope with the "bogey of authenticity."[7] By discussing epistemological and ontological vantage points, I would at best, learn that "Indigenous research is a humble and humbling activity"[8], and at worst, I may amuse people by "the gymnastics of theoretical language – hegemony and subalternity indeed…".[9] Moreover, after we ask "What is northeastern folk literature in India?" or "When would one mark the earliest period of north eastern folk literatures?" other questions await us: "What is folk literature?" or "What is period?" or "What is literature?" Definitive answers to these questions would inevitably lead to a 'validation' of folk literatures on being 'heard' as marginalized voices using established theory and irrelevant aesthetics.

The premise of misunderstanding and misreading could have been a deterrent to my readings in north eastern folk literatures had I not read the remarks of the then Honourable Speaker of Arunachal Pradesh, Tako Dabi in his "Inaugural Address" to a two-day national seminar on "Oral Literature of North-east India with special reference to Arunachal Pradesh" organized by Sahitya Akademi, Baroda:

> A truly brotherly attitude towards this region and scholarly studies in North-Eastern region would make us feel more akin to the rest of the country which would make everybody know how much, we the tribal and non-tribal people of this region, contributed for the growth and development of an Indian culture and thereby an Indian mind in the North-Eastern corner of our country.[10]

Therefore, I believe as a Bengali woman living in Calcutta, reading north-eastern folk literatures has some 'stake' in it for me as well. I choose not only to form a collective dialogue of marginalized voices but also to fathom how writing and storytelling are "powers" which can be "tapped in ways that are both spiritually nourishing and politically effective."[11]

In the manner of describing oneself through multifarious

identities, a note of 'emotional' and hence, faulty 'reasoning' may be discerned, the kind that must distance itself from any 'serious' academic treatise, or one that is not 'intellectually coherent and critically informed'. Often, in academia, a confluence of 'personal' and 'private' encounters in readings of concerned texts may be criticized. A formal academic conference requires, with due justification, seriousness of thought and enterprise, and therefore, personal experiences introduce an undesirable sense of 'frivolity'. However, one may have reservations in considering academic work to be untouched by personal experience. With comparatist, Ipshita Chanda, I recognize that "Any kind of expression....that uses words as medium, whether written or oral, is wittingly or unwittingly, a record of the encounter between life histories and the historical moment, and thus any text is a testimony of this encounter."[12] My readings in north-eastern folk literatures must be informed by the above-mentioned 'identities', which themselves are in flux since the "real space of modern life consists of heterotopias."[13] Also, in my readings in north-eastern folk literature, I would like to learn how literature has its own means and methods of rendering these encounters into literary works within a literary system. As an academician in the context of an urban English-speaking metropolis, one often functions within a system of thought which wishes to categorize, label, and name. Naming is a site of authority. Any portion of reality which is not tangible is deemed as 'fantasy', as 'non-analytical' and hence, deserving of condescending patronage at the most. A story can never be 'real'. However, as Kynpham Sing Nongkynrih mentions in his "Prelude" to *Around the Hearth: Khasi Legends*,

> It is very important [...] to understand the allegorical nature of the stories, so that they are not simply read as fantastic tales from yet another exotic tribal culture.[14]

Storytelling, then, is an inseparable part of the web of life, and an expression of experience, rather than only a reflection of the same. Words are sacrosanct and are not objects to be wasted. Therefore, story through words represents the epistemological and ontological basis of indigenous thought processes. Knowledge, teachings, humour, spirituality are elements of life which become integral to north-eastern folklore. Storytelling then becomes a powerful weapon of subversion, of protest, representing the power of man in shaping reality through language. Language becomes a metaphor for potential change. So-called mainstream ideology has been sustained by a continuous negation of indigenous notions of history. This was because more than often, such views were considered 'primitive', 'incorrect', and also ones which subverted and revolted against the colonial machinery. Stories within the fabric of north-eastern folklore provide the theoretical framework of their writing.

I would like to focus on the 'trickster' figure, in particular, in north-eastern folklore. The ambivalent trickster figure (known as Tentan, Matsuo or in the form of various animal figures such as the fox, the monkey or a jackal) allows for a resilient chameleon-like persona, capable of fluidity in form and character and hence capable, by extension, of formulating alter/counter histories for marginalized peoples. Trickster tales position a "trinity" of "asking, listening, and hearing"[15] which entails a non-indigenous reader to become the trickster, to draw his/her own lessons from the story, only if s/he wishes to. It is always open-ended. This does not imply that such stories encourage dilettantism, or anarchy in thought. But, then what is going on here?

The folktale is often considered to be a travelling metaphor, which finds new meaning with each new telling. The trickster figure is often subversive as the underdog, and amoral in terms of ethics. S/he, often a wily rogue, is a survivor in the face of any kind of adversity. Tentan tales of the wily village rogue is found in tales of Kacharis, Miris, and the Meches. Similar to Tentan is the character of Apfuho in Lhota Naga tales. Though the characters are mutually exclusive, they do share a distinct kinship. A similar story of guile and survival is told through the tale of Matsuo, the trickster in Angami tales. Matsuo through various incidents is able to supersede his fellow villagers. The trickster figure is thus ambivalent in its very dexterity. The stories represent not merely deceit and guile, but enlighten oneself about methods of survival utilizing industrious and enterprising resourcefulness. The figure of the trickster offers itself to myths, explanatory tales, romantic tales, tales of the formula type and humorous tales. According to Praphulladatta Goswami,

> The trickster sort of symbolizes the pleasure which is felt when a clever person inflicts discomfitures on dupes and fools and thus causes laughter.[16]

Essentially good-humoured, the trickster tales reflect a protest against any kind of orthodoxy and hierarchical powers. The trickster carries the power between diverse worldviews. It is not a static or conceptually tidy link between two kinds of world of which one is a part. Rather, it goes beyond such links on an epistemological, ontological basis and captures the rhythm of evolution beyond the individuals who carry the evolution forward. Therefore, the trickster is bestowed with sociopolitical significance and plays a distinct role in the evolution of human society. The trickster may also be viewed as a harbinger of change and transformation. As a transformer character, it highlights one of the crucial aspects within folk literatures, the theme of transformation. The transformer character communicates values which are linked to Indigenous cultures, sociopolitical realities, and community values. Praphulladatta Goswami notes that transformation of a person or a natural object into a human being is an integral feature of folk literature.

One notices not only the transformation of characters but a story of accommodation, negotiation and understanding. In the art of storytelling, the listener/reader is expected to participate. Therefore, in order to engage in an intercultural dialogue, it becomes imperative to read history from the indigenous perspective, and then formulate one's own responses rooted in particular cultural ethos. Perhaps, dialogue may facilitate "moral accountability", "responsible scholarship" and personalized literary criticism.[17] Through responses evolved in reading and from the texts, the reader indeed becomes the trickster, an agent of great social transformations.

Perhaps, it is also the image of the trickster which enables and encourages contemporary writers to create characters who are resourceful, vibrant and tenacious. The 'trickster' in the context of north-eastern folklore has a nuanced dimension, and a certain degree of ambivalence. Trickster-like qualities are developed through survival in the face of life and death. By focusing on a contemporary Ao Naga short story by Temsula Ao, "The Jungle Major", we discover similar characters that survive, persevere and in this particular instance, prosper. Resilience, in the form of humour, attachment to land, performance, and a projection of a trickster spirit, offers a source of optimism and hope in the short story. The protagonists embark on a journey of self-discovery and understanding, because they are both passionate about a quest for an ideal which would not assimilate them into mainstream popular culture. The short story is not only historical in its content but may also be read as 'travel narrative' emblematic as a gesture of performance. Performance is integral to human agency and culture. In the process, the narrative achieves a degree of complexity which challenges any kind of hegemonic reading into the oeuvre.

The story, "The Jungle Major" is part of a collection by Temsula Ao in a book entitled *These Hills Called Home: Stories from a War Zone.* The stories cover half a century of bloodshed that has marked the troubled history of Nagaland. The struggles of the people for an independent Nagaland and their continuing search for identity provide the backdrop for the stories. The stories describe how ordinary people cope with violence, how they negotiate power and force, how they seek and find safe spaces and enjoyment in the midst of terror. Dedicated to "those who know what we have done to ourselves", the book speaks of a "tremendous responsibility" which compels one to share "collective experience" in order to "teach the living how not to die".[18]

"The Jungle Major"[19] which is the first story in the collection begins "In the pre-dawn warmth of togetherness" where two mismatched lovers are making love "with the fervor of lovers meeting after a long absence".[20] Punaba, a nondescript and ugly looking humble driver from a minor clan in the village marries the elegant and beautiful Khatila belonging to a relatively well established and respected clan. The chagrined villagers are however silenced by the equanimity between the couple, who live a simple domestic life after marriage. The couple is childless and the village gossip entertains more speculation on the mismatched pair. However, the couple "appeared to be totally absorbed in each other and their own household."[21] The idyllic state of affairs, almost a fairytale picture of Khatila in the farms and of Punaba in his everyday work schedule as a driver continues till "the entire land was caught in the new wave of patriotic fervour that swept the imagination of the people and plunged them into a struggle which many did not even understand."[22] The fervour infects the village as well and Punaba finds himself involved in the underground activities of protest. When government officials come to question Khatila and the villagers about Punaba, Khatila maintains an apparently nonchalant attitude. She consistently guiles the interrogating officials by claiming that not only did she not know where her husband was, but did not care if he returned or not.

> Judging from the description of the man given by the gaonbura, the officer concluded that a beautiful woman like her could not be heartbroken over the disappearance of an insignificant man like Punaba from her life.[23]

As entire villages are ravaged by government officials and innocent villagers prosecuted for supposed acts of treason, Khatila maintains a trickster kind of resilience. Unassuming, and often insignificant within the main context of village decisions, she is yet a steady force which follows her husband's career in the underground army with avid interest. Punaba on his part arranges for secret meetings with his wife, bypassing authoritarian surveillance. However, in one such visit, Punaba is left in a tight corner. The authorities, he hears, would be arriving for an inspection of their small bamboo and thatch house. Apparently, there is no way of escape.

> Khatila was in a quandary, what could she do? How could she save her husband, herself and the entire village from the approaching soldiers?[24]

Like the transformer character in folklore, Khatila too transforms herself and her husband in the fraction of a second.

> ...she fished out some of her husband's old clothes and

> ordered him to get into them, then she smeared his face, hands and feet with ash from the hearth, hid his sandals, ruffled his hair and began shouting at him, 'You no good loafer, what were you doing all day yesterday? There is no water in the house even to wash my face. Run to the well immediately or you will rue the day you were born.'[25]

While shouting, Khatila continues to empty the water vessels in the house at the backyard. The investigating officer is chagrined at meeting "a disheveled but defiant person who displayed no agitation and seemed to be utterly oblivious to any danger" instead of "a cowering woman, crazy with fear for her husband and herself."[26] The humble and quiet housewife turns into a querulous shrew in front of the investigating officer. Moreover, as soon as she boldly summarily dismisses the servant (her husband in disguise) to safety in front of the officer, she further transforms into a coy woman offering tea. Almost tongue-in-cheek, she mentions that she could at least "get that much water from her neighbour" to make tea for the officer. The officer who is bedazzled by Khatila's beauty is sanguine that someone as ugly as the scurrying servant cannot be the husband of the beautiful village girl. The officer underestimates the audacity of the village girl, her presence of mind and instinct for survival. The joke is eventually at the cost of official powers. Eventually, Punaba achieves greater heights in the underground army by dint of his skill and leadership qualities and is promoted to the rank of a Major. When the government announces a ceasefire, Punaba comes overground upon Khatila's insistence. He is given a job in the State Transport Department as a mechanic and is posted at Mokokchung.

> The story of the couple is then passed on by word of mouth amongst friends, and retold over and over again as a metaphor for resourcefulness and bravery.
>
> Every time the story was recounted, Punaba would look at his wife and ask playfully, 'Aren't you glad that your jungle major is so ugly?" And equally playfully, she would answer, 'So, where is the water I sent you to fetch that day?'[27]

The story of Punaba and Khatila remains embedded in

both collective and individual memory and becomes a part of collective-community knowledge. As performance previously delivered through word-of-mouth, it has been stored, preserved and transmitted through memory. Such performance gains the status of heightened forms of communication, and forms the basis of collective consciousness till there is another performance. Performance also involves an instantaneous audience, since what the audience brings to its memory completes performance. Oratory is a language that conveys "passion, emotion, and character" whether spoken or written down. The spontaneity and feeling in an oral communication bespeaks an inherited wisdom. Human dignity and existence is predicated on the ability to sustain wisdom through the ages. Theory is conveyed through sharing of stories and not through obtuse academic jargon. Perhaps, one of the best ways of expression of stories is folklore which "is perhaps as old as mankind."[28] A folktale is often seen as a travelling metaphor which finds a new meaning with each new telling. In many instances, folktales are also related to material culture involving techniques, skills, recipes and formulas which are passed down from generation to generation displaying unique modes of survival and understandings. For example, a story in this collection entitled, "The Pot Maker" revolves around the story of a little girl in an Ao Naga community initiated in the art of pot making. The story reveals how pot making is an art practiced by expert women pot makers for the sake of their communities' sustenance and survival. However, the art is a hazardous one given the geographical conditions for the collection of the right clay and the painstaking labour involved in the same. This is why the mother of the young girl in the story refuses to teach her daughter the art. Sentila's mother's refusal to teach her daughter and the latter's determination to master the art draw the attention of the village elders. The elders summon Sentila's father for questioning and remind him that "skills such as pot making, which not only catered to the needs of the people but also symbolized the tradition and history of the people did not 'belong' to any individual. And experts were obliged to pass on their skills not only to their own children but also to anyone who wished to learn."[29] The father is made to realize that the village follows the policy of greater good for the community rather than adhering to individual predilections. The daughter is therefore initiated into the art of pot making by a reluctant mother. However, Sentila is unable to perform well as far as the shaping of the models is concerned. Her mother's open disdain towards her clumsiness further aggravates matters.

The whole process seemed to have become a contest where the mother's will seemed to thwart every attempt of the despairing daughter to create even the semblance of a pot out of the recalcitrant clay.[30]

As Sentila continues to produce 'misshapen parodies' instead of her 'dream pots', she reaches puberty and as per community rules, has to spend the night in one of the girls' dormitories. It is here that under the gentle guidance of the presiding matron, or Onula (Aunt) that the young girl learns the basics of the art, albeit secretly. Onula, as we find, is drawn to Sentila because the story of the discord of mother and daughter had already reached her ears, as a part of collective village knowledge. Moreover, she makes it clear to Sentila that the real skill must be passed on from mother to daughter rather than in any other fashion.

It is not from me that you should receive this knowledge. It is your mother who has to pass it on to you. Remember, the village has ruled.[31]

In the next pot making session, according to Onula's advice, Sentila watches her mother's work more closely. The mother observes but is silent at her daughter's eye for detail. On a sunny morning, the mother takes her daughter for another pot making session. She leaves the work table after finishing her batch and asks Sentila to make another batch of pots. Sentila is surprised at her mother's assumption that the girl would be able to make decent pots and the fact that she leaves the working shed rather than staying over to gloat over the child's clumsiness. What follows is Sentila's miraculous ability to make almost identical beautiful pots such as that of her mother. On returning home for lunch, Sentila finds her mother mysteriously dead. Throughout the wake, Sentila remains speechless, refusing to touch food or drink. It is only the next morning when the body was being carried out that she cries:

> Mother, I did not wish it to happen this way; it simply came to me. Please forgive me.[32]

Her remarks carry no significance to anyone but to Onula, one of the mourners present. She realizes that something momentous had transformed both mother and daughter at life's appointed hour on that fateful day.[33]

A glance at the identical batches of pots inside the work shed makes Onula realize that "A new pot maker was born."[34] How does one account for such mysterious miracles? What does Sentila mean by stating 'it simply came to me'? Perhaps, her mother's death is evocative of the stringent rules of a community which insist that gifts must be passed on from mother to daughter. Also, does Sentila attain trickster like qualities – that of a great transformer – with the ability to bring forward momentous change? Perhaps, the figure of the trickster becomes even more crucial if one takes into consideration the ongoing journey upon which the trickster embarks. The point is not merely to seek answers to questions, but to reaffirm one's niche within a distinct community with specific cultural roots. Moreover, "The Pot Maker" insists through its specific rhythmic structure and syntax that the story be read aloud such that the reader becomes the trickster. Resilience, in the form attachment to earth-bound skills, mothering, and a projection of a trickster spirit, offers a source of optimism and hope.

Storytelling then becomes a powerful weapon of subversion, of protest. An old saying goes thus: "Birds do not sing because they have answers, birds sing because they have songs." The hegemony of epistemology is such that too much authority is given to 'knowledge'. In the process of reading/ listening to these "stories from a war zone", to assume to have taken the "absolutely"[35] right approach to the same would be dangerous, if not foolish. The fact is that 'literary criticism' is itself insulting to the indigenous condition as no one may assume to know the absolute meaning of any work of art. Hence, positioning oneself vis-à-vis these writings becomes controversial if one were to travel from theory to practice. Rather, a *rapprochement* (a site of negotiation, of exchange) may be attempted between the two by travelling from the texts to their specific historical locations. Theory would be worked upon *a posteriori*. Therefore any journey into such 'contemporary transformations' cannot begin from preconceived theoretical practices; rather the theories may be developed through the words of the writers themselves. Their texts, stories would give an understanding on how one may read them. One also realizes that linguistic understanding is only one case of understanding and not an exhaustive one. Therefore, understanding must be articulated outside linguistic understanding. The dynamics of epistemology involves a notion of equilibrium generated by a 'self which understands'. Discomfort arises automatically where one attempts to 'know' in a situation where knowledge and understanding are both fragmented. "An Old Man Remembers" begins with the death of the old man Sashi's childhood friend, Imli. The reader is informed of the close bond between the two childhood friends including their association with the underground movement as comrades-in-arms. Sashi's final address to his friend as the latter lay in his coffin is one which is replete with multiple stories of togetherness. Sashi says:

> So Imli, after all, you've decided to leave me and go ahead, ha. When we were young, I could outrun you any time, but today you have overtaken me. But, no matter, such time is not of our choosing. Go in peace, my friend and do not look back. I, too, shall cross the water soon and join you. Until then, Kuknalim![36]

The people at the funeral realize that Sashi's voice sounds young and firm and without the usual lisp on account of missing teeth and old age. They are also surprised to see him stand erect, in spite of his bad leg ("everyone knew he had a bad leg"). The community is indeed an integral part of the lives of these two old men. The dualism of a literary text is usually based on the meaning of the text and authorial intention. The structure and context of a text such as "An Old Man Remembers" deconstructs the dualism and converges social and literary history. It also draws attention to the space of the 'text' which is not 'fixed' or 'finite', much to the unease of mainstream critics and intellectuals. The words 'spoken' attain a newer theoretical dimension, vastly different from printed two-dimensional words. Therefore, Sashi's reminiscences on the past are punctured by a question from his grandson:

> Grandfather, is it true that you and grandfather Imli killed many people when you were in the jungle?[37]

The question leads to the formulation of a mythic history mapped under real territory and geography. It leads to an understanding of truth as capacity to recognize. Sashi relives the painful struggles of the 1950s in Nagaland as part of an underground group of activists. The contemporary act of storytelling is a complicated one. It has a twofold function. Primarily, through its immediate role of 'narration' within a written format, it gives a sense of 'being-told-to' as in verbal storytelling. Secondly, it also gains significance as a written art preserved for posterity. At all junctions, 'storytelling' involves a complex process of expressing the significance of language through a narration of the events (plot) and also draws attention to multiple narrative strands across translucent borders of cultural paradigms. Sashi ponders:

> Did he have the right to keep youngsters like his own grandson in the dark about the price their parents and grandparents had paid for a piece of the earth they now called Nagaland? But where would he begin? Should he begin by saying, 'When I was young like you?'But had he ever been given a chance to be young like them?[38]

The old man finally decides to narrate the stories of the war time, the atrocities and oppression faced by Naga youth in post-Independence India. Interestingly, the horrors of his underground days are interspersed with one of a 'fantastic adventure' (shared with Imli) of surreptitiously watching a naked woman amongst a group of women after bathing. The old man realizes that instead of chuckling over that experience with his grandson, he speaks of the 'areas of darkness' in his life. Perhaps, the concept of rationality is held ransom to epistemology. Furthermore, what is finally related to truth means and ends to what is cognitive. Having told his story, he tells his grandson:

> I do not know if what I have told you answers your question or makes you understand your reasons for asking it. But there is nothing more I can add. You have to make what you can from what I have tried to tell you.[39]

The Old Man achieves his goal through the reflection of truth, an inheritance of words of power which he feels morally obligated to transmit to his grandson. The fluidity of language perpetuates a continuous narrative. The agency of listening is significant since rather than the protagonists asserting their individual voices, it is the land which speaks through them. It therefore becomes imperative to be a keen listener to the stories emanating from the language which in turn is rooted in the land. The stories must be retold correctly, in accurate form for the sake of a rethinking of history, devoid of power inequalities.

"The Jungle Major" or "The Pot Maker" or "An Old Man Remembers", therefore, tend to bypass hegemonic normative labels vis-à-vis what should constitute 'literature' and by extension, combats an insidious multiculturalism which has intruded into mainstream reading practices. To use the approach of Gayatri Chakraborty Spivak, one of the leading scholars of postcolonialism, one need not be 'indigenous' to a culture in order to read a "culturally different book" and in fact, "To think the contrary is to fetishize national origin and deny the historical production of the colonial subject."[40]

I had felt that one had to justify her vantage point by answering the questions posed to her. One did not realize that by demanding answers from oneself, one was actually becoming a prey to the discourse, which thinks in binaries, of good/bad, white/black, marginalized/dominant, and thus offering a simplistic and neat ending to all. One was searching for a 'happy ending' to the story. By insisting upon a *telos*, one was unwittingly speaking through the discourse of 'imperialism' which is "tied to a chronology of events related to 'discovery', conquest, exploitation, distribution and appropriation." My subjective location offers a different but still an outsider's response as a 'reader'. Perhaps, it is possible to actually question the concept of 'readership' itself, since folk literature to a great extent is based on a tradition of orality. 'To listen' becomes a crucial part of the ideology of folk literature. The emphasis is on the agency of listening. The 'reader' thus becomes the 'listener' who is able to enact, unwittingly perhaps, the politics of difference implicated in folk literature. This would eventually lead to an epistemological and ontological shift, whereby there may be material socio-political change. One may further elucidate the point within the discursive framework of the text itself. Admitting the dangers of conventional literary criticism, the stories apprehend a scholarship which would involve both traditional academic and non-traditional, non-academic forms of knowledge. The binary of the traditional and the non-traditional, or more specifically the academic and the non-academic actually reveals an unwillingness to accept ontological and epistemological truths that differ from what has been traditionally passed down. It, therefore, negates positionality as a fluid entity, open to change, transition and dialogue between cultures.

Gestures of love, respect and passion abound in these stories. Humour also becomes a powerful tool of encountering deep-rooted grief and anger against a dominant, patriarchal system in both political and personal fronts. It would therefore be incorrect to superimpose any fixed literary theory upon such writings. For instance, a postcolonial thrust would subsume the basic premise of folk literature with its deep connections to land, language, and all life manifested in different forms. Writing involves the process of transforming stories into an alien language, and yet retaining the multi-dimensionality of indigenous lives. However, a single text cannot be considered to be the prototype for an entire community. A text is not an anthropological artifact, or document. It is a work of literary aesthetics, which provokes us to open our eyes to another world, invests meanings and further dimensions to our skills as literary scholars. In the expression of filial affections, and ties of blood and community, the literary work encapsulates experienced events aesthetically. This is turn mobilizes future possibilities of change and transformation.

NOTES

1. Smith, Linda Tuhiwai. *Decolonizing Methodologies: Research and Indigenous Peoples*, Dunedin: London and New York and University of Otago Press, 1999, p. 1.
2. Eigenbrod, Renate. *Travelling Knowledges: Positioning the Im/ Migrant Reader of Aboriginal Literatures in Canada*, Winnipeg: University of Manitoba Press, 2005, p. 24.
3. Said, Edward. *Orientalism*, London: Vintage Books, 1978, p. 2.
4. Dev, Amiya, "Literary History from Below", in Amiya Dev and Sisir Kumar Das eds., *Comparative Literature: Theory and* Practice, Shimla: Indian Institute of Advanced Study, 1989, 326
5. *Ibid.*, p. 326.
6. Razack, Sherene H. *Looking White People in the Eye: Gender, Race and Culture in Courtrooms and Classrooms*, Toronto: U of Toronto P, 1998, p. 10.
7. Rushdie, Salman. *Imaginary Homelands'* New York: Penguin Books, 1991, p. 67.
8. Smith, p. 5.
9. King, Thomas. *The Truth About Stories: A Native Narrative* Minneapolis: University of Minnesota, 2003, p. 115.
10. Dabi, Tako. "Inaugural Address" in *Folk Culture and Oral Literature from North-East India*, edited by Tamo Mibang & Sarit K. Chaudhuri, New Delhi: Mittal Publications, 2004, p. 11.
11. Marlatt, Daphne. "Introduction: Meeting on Fractured Margins", in *Telling It: Women and Language Across Cultures*, ed. Sky Lee, Lee Maracle, Daphne Marlatt, and Betsy Warland, Vancouver: Press Gang Publishers, 1990, p. 13.
12. Chanda, Ipshita. *Literary Historiography: Literary Studies in India,* Kolkata: DSA, Department of Comparative Literature, Jadavpur University, 2004.
13. Chatterjee, Partha. *The Politics of the Governed,* New York: Columbia University Press, 2004, p. 7.
14. Kynpham Sing Nongkynrih, "Prelude" in *Around the Hearth: Khasi Legends,* Delhi: Penguin Books, 2007, p. x.
15. Hoy, Helen. *How Should I Read These? Native Women Writers in Canada,* Toronto: University of Toronto Press, 2001, p. 35.

16. Goswami, Praphulladatta, "Naga Tales", *Essays on the Folklore and Culture of North-Eastern India*, Gauhati: Spectrum Publications, 1983, p. 49.
17. *Ibid.*, p. 99.
18. Ao, Temsula. "Lest We Forget" in *These Hills Called Home: Stories from a War Zone* (New Delhi: Penguin Books in association with Zubaan, 2006), p. x.
19. Ao, Temsula. "The Jungle Major" in *These Hills Called Home: Stories from a War Zone* (New Delhi: Penguin Books in association with Zubaan, 2006), p. 1.
20. *Ibid.*, p. 1.
21. *Ibid.*, p. 2.
22. *Ibid.*, pp. 2-3.
23. *Ibid.*, p. 4.
24. *Ibid.*, p. 5.
25. *Ibid.*, p. 6.
26. *Ibid.*, p. 6.
27. *Ibid.*, p. 7.
28. Handoo, Jawaharlal. "Folklore and Folklife: An Introduction", in *Folklore in North-East India*. ed. Soumen Sen, New Delhi: Omsons Publications, 1985, 1-16, p. 1.
29. Ao, Temsula. "The Pot maker" in *These Hills Called Home: Stories from a War Zone,* New Delhi: Penguin Books in association with Zubaan, 2006, p. 62.
30. *Ibid.*, p. 63.
31. Ao, Temsula. "The Pot maker" in *These Hills Called Home: Stories from a War Zone,* New Delhi: Penguin Books in association with Zubaan, 2006, p. 65.
32. *Ibid.*, p. 67.
33. *Ibid.*, p. 67.
34. *Ibid.*, p. 68.
35. I am inspired here by Japanese Canadian writer Joy Kogawa's comment, "I don't think we ever absolutely know whether we're doing the right thing or not. We just sort of stumble to the right, and we stumble to the left, and we struggle, and that's what it

means to be part of the human condition." Joy Kogawa, in "From the Bottom of the Well, From the Distant Stars, in *Telling It: Women and Language Across Cultures*, Ed. Sky Lee et al. Vancouver: Press Gang Publishers, 1990, p. 97.

36. Ao, Temsula. "An Old Man Remembers" in *These Hills Called Home: Stories from a War Zone,* New Delhi: Penguin Books in association with Zubaan, 2006, p. 90.

37. *Ibid.*, p. 92.

38. Ao, Temsula. "An Old Man Remembers" in *These Hills Called Home: Stories from a War Zone,* New Delhi: Penguin Books in association with Zubaan, 2006, p. 93.

39. *Ibid.*, p. 112.

40. Spivak, Gayatri. "How to Read a 'Culturally Different' Book," in *Colonial Discourse/ Postcolonial Theory*, ed. Francis Barker, Peter Hulm, and Margaret Iverson, Manchester and New York: Manchester University Press, 1994, p. 143.

REFERENCES

Ao, Temsula, "Lest We Forget" in *These Hills Called Home: Stories from a War Zone,* New Delhi: Penguin Books in association with Zubaan, 2006.

Ao, Temsula, "The Jungle Major" in *These Hills Called Home: Stories from a War Zone,* New Delhi: Penguin Books in association with Zubaan, 2006.

Ao, Temsula, "An Old Man Remembers" in *These Hills Called Home: Stories from a War Zone,* New Delhi: Penguin Books in association with Zubaan, 2006.

Ao, Temsula, "The Pot Maker" in *These Hills Called Home: Stories from a War Zone,* New Delhi: Penguin Books in association with Zubaan, 2006.

Baym, Nina. *Novels, Readers, and Reviewers,* Ithaca, NY: Cornell UP, 1984.

Chanda, Ipshita *Literary Historiography: Literary Studies in India,* Kolkata: DSA, Department of Comparative Literature, Jadavpur University, 2004.

Chatterjee, Partha *The Politics of the Governed,* New York: Columbia University Press, 2004.

Dabi, Tako, "Inaugural Address" in Tamo Mibang & Sarit K. Chaudhuri (ed.) *Folk Culture and Oral Literature from North-East India*, New Delhi: Mittal Publications, 2004.

Dev, Amiya "Literary History from Below", in Amiya Dev and Sisir Kumar Das eds., *Comparative Literature: Theory and* Practice, Shimla: Indian Institute of Advanced Study, 1989.

Eigenbrod, Renate "Can 'The Subaltern' Be Read? The Role of the Critic in Postcolonial Studies. An Epilogue to a Workshop." Tobias Doring, Uwe Schafer, and Mark Stein. (ed.) *Can 'The Subaltern' Be Read?* Frankfurt: Institut fur England und Amerikastudien, 1996, pp. 97-101.

Eigenbrod, Renate *Travelling Knowledges: Positioning the Im/Migrant Reader of Aboriginal Literatures in Canada*, Winnipeg: University of Manitoba Press, 2005.

Goswami, Praphulladatta "Naga Tales", *Essays on the Folklore and Culture of North-Eastern India*, Gauhati: Spectrum Publications, 1983.

Handoo, Jawaharlal. "Folklore and Folklife: An Introduction", in Soumen Sen (ed.) *Folklore in North-East India*. New Delhi: Omsons Publications, 1985, 1-16.

Hooks, Bell. *Black Looks: Race and Representation*. Boston: South End, 1992.

Hoy, Helen. *How Should I Read These? Native Women Writers in Canada,* Toronto: University of Toronto Press, 2001.

King, Thomas. *The Truth About Stories: A Native Narrative,* Minneapolis: University of Minnesota, 2003.

Maracle, Lee, *Oratory: Coming to Theory* (North Vancouver: Gallerie, 1990).

Marlatt, Daphne "Introduction: Meeting on Fractured Margins", in Sky Lee, et al. *Telling It: Women and Language Across Cultures*, Vancouver: Press Gang Publishers, 1990.

Nongkynrih, Kynpham Sing. "Prelude" in *Around the Hearth: Khasi Legends,* Delhi: Penguin Books, 2007,

Rushdie, Salman. *Imaginary Homelands,* New York: Penguin Books, 1991.

Said, Edward, *Orientalism,* London: Vintage Books, 1978.

Sherene H. Razack, *Looking White People in the Eye: Gender, Race and Culture in Courtrooms and Classrooms*, Toronto: U of Toronto P, 1998.

Smith, Linda Tuhiwai *Decolonizing Methodologies: Research and Indigenous Peoples,* Dunedin: London and New York and University of Otago Press, 1999.

Spivak, Gayatri. "How to Read a 'Culturally Different' Book," in ed. Francis Barker, Peter Hulm, and Margaret Iverson, (ed.) *Colonial Discourse/Postcolonial Theory*, Manchester and New York: Manchester University Press, 1994.

10

A Study of Selected Old Sayings and Narratives of the Mizo: Oral Literature as Knowledge System

Margaret Ch. Zama

In this day and age of globalization, when boundaries of knowledge and culture have become blurred, where we share pressing global concerns such as environmental challenges of global warming, air and water pollution; where global climatic changes and the implications they carry are forecast, there has arisen the urgent need to delve into, and project indigenous knowledge systems of communities that could contribute alternatives to save the environment. Though such knowledge systems may not be detected in the following study of old Mizo sayings and narratives, yet the innate wisdom of a tribal community that contributed to its survival as well as the laying of a strong foundation for universal moral values throughout its many generations, cannot be denied.

It is hoped that this brief study will contribute in its own way, to 'a new vision for the study of literature focusing on its entity as a cognitive system that has its own dynamics of knowing and making'. It will be seen that the case studies taken up in this paper contain knowledge systems pertaining to everyday living for a highly insular tribal community, yet possessing larger world-views which cannot remain unique to its culture alone.

One of the sources of embedded and perhaps, in some cases,

hidden knowledge systems in a tribal community like the Mizo, lies in its rich oral tradition. Its nomadic lifestyle still considered recent in terms of history, and its pre-literate past just over a hundred and fourteen years old (having got their alphabet from the white missionaries in 1894), the Mizo ancestors appear to have been more preoccupied with their survival from wild beasts, disease and enemies, than in the pursuit of creative and aesthetic knowledge. In spite of this, the Mizo has a rich trove of oral narratives and songs wherein lies much of its socio-cultural history.

The Mizo continued to be nomadic as late as the 1890s, long after having arrived in their present homeland. Being an agrarian society dependant on the land they continually moved once in every four years approximately, in search of fertile ground once the resources of their present settlement were depleted. The old folk unable to work in the fields, stayed behind to keep an eye on things, and being the obvious repositories of whatever knowledge and age-old wisdom that the tribe had gleaned through the generations, took on the role of the 'teller of tales' as well as informal teacher to the young.

The fact that the Mizo societal setup was totally community-based, where the welfare and general good of the public took precedence over individuals and family units is reflected in many of its old sayings which are still quoted as guidelines for everyday living, and seen as the foundation of present-day Mizo ethics. Some examples are, *"The orphan and the community are ever supportive of each other"*, which bears the truth that the general public who carry no direct responsibility for an orphan, are nonetheless ever ready to sympathise with him against his caregivers. *Even the big boulder cannot survive without the support of the smaller stone; Being at war with one's neighbour is worse than being at war with seven villages; Share and survive, eat alone and perish* contain basic truths that all cultures can identify with. The last saying quoted here, has assumed of late an interesting politicization by becoming the standard cry against the corruption of politicians who fill their coffers with no thought or care for the rest of society. It is also reflective of the 'giving and sharing' culture of the old Mizo community whose survival was rooted in this principle. This can be further extended to include the well-known concept of *tlawmngaihna* which, simply put, is the selfless giving of oneself even unto disgrace or death, without expectation of returns. Again, a number of sayings contain surprising universal truths such as, *If one's aim is high, so also the fall; A deformed body or an ugly face cannot be helped, but character can be remedied; It is never late for deformity and leprosy to set in,* and so on. The old Mizo community was adamant to the point of superstition about one thing, which was never to despise the deformed or turn one's back on the needy or sick, for the same misfortune could befall anyone.

On the flip side, a few old sayings also reflect some negative traits of the society which reveal the mindset of a highly chauvinistic culture. A woman's lowly status is sadly reflected in some of them, some examples being, *Women and crabs have no character; A woman's wisdom does not extend beyond the public water point; Let a woman and a female dog with litter growl to their satisfaction; Old fences and old wives can be replaced.* Such sayings may be viewed as classic examples of strong gender biases ingrained in the male psyche. They perform the function of instructions however indirect, over women in the society. It is thus possible to study and view some knowledge systems as capable of containing and generating what may be considered negative, destructive motives and ends.

To come to the domain of tales and narratives, the Mizo have a unique collection of tales associated with the legendary Chhura who runs the gamut of roles from brother, husband, fool, trickster to culture hero. Fusing both positive and negative traits, he may be seen to reflect various aspects of the native Mizo mindset and nature. Chhura in some of the tales displays a lovable albeit foolish character, ready to fall victim to the manipulative ways of his kinsman Nahaia. Yet, in others, he can be as cunning and manipulative, resourceful and impudent, if not more so, than Nahaia. A rereading of these tales certainly contains the potential for new and relevant interpretations within the modern context. In allowing a reader to rebuild the texts so to say, we extend the particular and localized dimensions of the knowledge content, to expand and spill over to other dimensions related to the theme.

In social terms, some of Chhura's actions are aggressive, destructive and forbidden. This is seen in the tale which tells of how he tricked his enemies into drowning themselves in the river, a fate which they had in fact intended for him. Before accomplishing this, he added insult to injury by arousing their greed for riches with his clever lies about untold treasures that lay in the river-bed. He told his enemies that all they had to do was tie empty vessels round their waists to carry the treasures in, and jump into the river. Blinded by greed, his enemies failed to realize that the empty vessels when filled with water would weigh them down and thus drown them. That Chhura showed a total lack of morals here is true, but it must be remembered that he was drawing on all his wit and knowledge resource in order to survive and save his own skin. The tale goes on to tell us of how he went around the village dousing all the fires in the hearth of every home after he had convinced the womenfolk into leaving to meet their husbands due back from their treasure-hunt. On their return in the late evening from their futile errand, tired and cold from the pouring rain, they had no choice but to pay the price demanded for fire to rekindle their hearths, which was, to sleep with Chhura for he alone had a huge warm fire going. His revenge was thus complete.

It is believed by some that Chhura was fully aware of his kinsman Nahaia's manipulative ways, but simply tolerated him in order to avoid conflict. This is seen in a tale where his reply to Nahaia's invitation to dig yams together again, was a definite no. He said, "No thanks, I don't wish to see my yams change colour again when washed in the stream." The truth of the matter was that Nahaia was too lazy to put in the effort to dig for the full grown white bottomed yams, and had on an earlier occasion, dug only the smaller red topped ones closer to the surface. When he suggested washing them in the nearby stream, he promptly washed his upstream and deliberately let go of them so that they would end up with Chhura's yams. He then selected the big white-bottomed yams while Chhura unhappily ended up with the small red-topped ones. Besides the humour and projection of Chhura as victim and fool in the tale, we readers become wiser with the obvious lesson on how to dig for good yams!

To be sagacious and know what to do in times of trouble is a quality admired by the Mizo. The tale of the ogress and the horn of plenty reveal how crafty and shrewd Chhura is. This is seen in the manner in which he devises his plan to capture the ogress, and then outdoes her in cunning by threatening to let the village children make sport of her. The thought of being humbled thus and losing face before the very victims whom she used to frighten, is the worst possible nightmare for her. Chhuras's clever reading of her psychology had her begging for mercy and talking of ransom, and in this way he was able to possess her coveted horn of plenty.

Knowledge system can be detected and gleaned from a different perspective from the tale of *Chemtatrawta,* a humorous round tale that contains much more than bawdy humour and wit. Chemtatrawta, representative of the chauvinistic tribal male whose first concern is to see that his work tools, especially the *dao*, a large indigenous chopper, was ever sharp and work-worthy, haunched down on a stone to sharpen it. Engrossed, he did not notice a freshwater prawn creep up to suddenly nip his testicles. Angered by the pain and humiliation, he sprang up and with his dao, impulsively chopped off a nearby bamboo plant upon which a vine was entwined. The fruit, a bitter gourd called a 'khaum', spitefully fell down heavily on the coccyx of a wild fowl below. This set off a chain of events caused by anger and spite. The wild fowl furiously scattered and scratched at a nearby ant nest which in turn, provoked its inmates, the ants, into biting a wild boar relaxing in the vicinity, right between his hind quarters. The wild boar in anger uprooted a plantain tree where a bat had made its home. The bat in annoyance flew right up the trunk of an elephant who, in turn, spitefully went on a rampage and trampled on the home of an old woman. The old woman in a fit of temper went and defecated at the village water source. Seeing their water supply contaminated, the whole village raised an uproar and demanded an explanation from her.

The story does a rewind with her reply, "Why did the elephant have to destroy my home?" It finally rounds back to the initial culprit, the naughty prawn, who is brought before the village council court to account for its behaviour. Unable to justify itself and at a loss for words, all he could say was, "Er...er...if you throw me into the fire I will turn bright red for the enjoyment of children, but if you put me into the water, I will turn quite, quite pale." So the villagers followed his instructions, but as soon as he was put into the water, the cunning prawn regained his senses and exclaimed, "I'm in my own element, my parent's home!" and swiftly swam away, taking refuge inside a little underwater recess which no one could reach. Determined to punish him, the villagers kept poking at it with the stalk of a *hnahthial* plant. This, we are told, is why the prawn's mouth is frayed and rough-edged, while the hnahthial plant, cursed by the prawn, continues to sport a sprayed top.

It would not be too farfetched to state that a rereading of the tale throws up certain issues no less relevant today than some of the pressing concerns noted at the initial stage of this paper. The value and need for co-existence and respect for another's space is one such issue. None of the animals in the tale gives a second thought as to how their actions might affect the welfare of others, just as Chemtatrawta showed his irresponsibility by reacting the way he did. He could have immediately addressed the culprit at hand instead of taking it out on the bamboo nearby which set off a chain of events that eventually went beyond his control. Another aspect is the importance of civic sense and cleanliness. The old lady's behaviour was unforgivable and not to be tolerated. She was therefore summoned before the people's court for questioning.

The Mizo is not unique in possessing etiological tales, tales of how things began or originated. Some may perhaps even find similar echoes in tales of other tribes and communities. We know that fiber from the sago palm is excellent material for making the bowstring of traps as the white ant cannot eat or gnaw it. This knowledge supposedly originated from Vanhrikpa, who was elected by both man and beast, to rule over them judiciously. It was at his judicious advice too, that the *hnahthial* plant and the sun-grass exchanged places to grow, after which they both thrived luxuriantly. The sun-grass has grown ever since in sunny open spaces and hill slopes while the *hnahthial* thrives in low-lying valleys.

It was believed that originally, the bamboo plant could not withstand strong winds and kept breaking until *Vanhrikpa* solved its problem. He advised the bamboo plant to tie a piece of string at equal distance throughout its length. This would in turn become nodes and the knot of the string tied would turn into eyes of the node. In this way, the bamboo is believed to have become strong and firm and ever since, able to withstand strong winds. The Mizo believe that it was the humble earthworm who increased the volume of the earth by eating and defecating continuously, while the rat is credited with being the one who brought the paddy grain back to mankind from across the daunting *Tuihriam* waters. As reward he was promised permission to live in the granary itself and eat to his heart's content.

From the few case studies explored in this paper, the ideas projected through the tales may seem fantastic and farfetched at times, especially when viewed with our modern sensibilities; yet they also provide a form of communicating the development of knowledge that a particular community undergoes. This in turn, can contribute towards the wider study of interdisciplinary interface between literature and philosophy, and in a larger context between the humanities and sciences.

11

Ethnophilosophy: Conceptual Artefacts, Wisdom and Critique of Anthropocentrism in India's Northeast

Prasenjit Biswas

This paper aims at investigating the plurality of discursive *techne* in claims of identity by various tribes in order to understand the modes of inclusion within the representational domain of post-colonial India. As post-colonial India engages itself in contests over plurality and authenticity, the situation in India's Northeast calls for a foundational understanding of the life-world and worldviews of various tribes affirming a distinct self-identity. It can be observed that constructions of tribal identity base themselves primarily on a specific world-view with its intimate responsiveness towards the members of the tribes, albeit with an amount of 'universality' in the inner resources of discursive construction of the 'self'. But this directedness towards oneself most often derives its 'intentional contents' from 'representations' of the Other without being necessarily distinguished from the Other. *This directedness essentially produces an erasure of both self and other in an entanglement within a shared space.*[1] This *erasure* takes the form of a monologue that does not listen to the Other, but imbricates the Other in a trajectory of simultaneous openness and closure.[2] One can characterize this process of opening and closing as a dialogic encounter with the Other which is paradoxically inter-cultural as well as ascriptive of a strong sense of difference with the Other. This trajectory cannot be understood without taking into account the presence of many singular worldviews that exhibits a closure to the Other, while many such worldviews collated together in a common space usher in a plurality with distinct shades within it. The question that can be investigated here is how such apparently windowless monadic worldviews interact with each other and how such an interaction affects openness between structures and identities. Where lies the agency of opening before the closure? In order to locate such an agency, *one has to examine the moments of colonization and decolonization of tribal mind through the 'conceptual artefacts' indigenous to a naturalized tribal identity.* Such artefacts of the mind project a self-enclosed identity outside itself and thereby turn the essential self-identity into an identity-in-difference to itself.[3] For a concrete grasp of the scenario, this paper proposes to take some such 'generic' tribal identities of India's Northeast such as Khasi, Apatani, Ao and Angami in order to understand the origins and trajectories of identity construction. In doing so, the paper aims to evolve a hermeneutic *strategy of recovery* from the lost terrains of historical and temporal sense of being that finds its closure within contemporary language games. Such lost terrains consist of (a) an originary sense of a place and the subsequent loss of the place and (b) the construction of an Other as an antithesis to the self in the form of racism, xenophobia and other such forms of violence.

The Idea of Northeast

The idea of the Northeast conceived as a frontier space, right through the colonial to the post-colonial served the purpose of state-building in terms of a 'differentiated, describable and enumerable' populace inhabiting 'non-state' spaces in the hills that lacked the presence of modern forms of biopower. This 'monochromatic' and 'ocular' space gave rise to a sense of ethnic and cultural othering that grew out of a nascent Indian self expelling its anxieties, contradictions and irrationalities onto the subalterns in the periphery in terms of being 'suspects' without any authentic sense of belonging. At times of crisis such as the immediate after-effects of Partition, such an othering of the Northeast was violently reversed by these people by an assumption of agency that can react and contest through an inherent conflictual circumstance. The very characterization of the political and social space of the Northeast in nationalist parlance turned out to be an act of exteriorization or Othering, which got transfigured and transgressed into a vengeance for the Other in the Northeast. This Cartesian division between a national self and an Other not only remained confined between the dominant and the subordinate, but got replicated within the Northeast in terms of dominant and non-dominant Others. Such an essentially contested Northeastern social space circumscribed itself on its internally coherent and meaningfully organized life-world leaving a different vantage to describe them in their own terms. These terms are a mix of life-world conceptual artifacts and articulation of a response to the so called 'mainstream' Indian national identity.

Such a mix is experiential. There are examples of such a mix when a Naga girl from Manipur cannot recollect her school days without talking about the 'fight' that was going on all around between the Army and the insurgents. The problematic of trauma and its psychical effects that is central to experience of time, the 'real time' that carries the trace of the unrepresentable beneath what one related to in the immediate. Phenomenal apprehension of time, therefore, opens towards the 'unrepresentable' expressed in language. In the context of the Northeast, when Mamang Dai says, 'we descend from solitudes and miracles'.[4] she means the trace of the unrepresentable that the Naga girl assumes to know herself. One can understand the situation in terms of return to a 'sublime and ungrounded' dimension of 'lived experience' that often assumes a discursive understanding of the 'self' in terms of a conceptually imagined 'continuum' between the past and the present, the self and the other. The continuum is multiply realized such as in sacred symbols and profane spaces. To exemplify momentarily, the Naga tribes such as Lhota, Sumi, Angami, Rengma believe themselves to have originated from the rock called *Khezakhenoma* which forms a conceptual continuum with Ao Nagas symbolizing village states in the form of monoliths that metaphorically alter their primordiality. The continuum gets further manifested in the use of various kinds of thread-square symbols near the graves to catch heavenly flies that may disturb the spirits of the dead. Such thread-square symbols are found among the Kachins of Myanmar as well as among the Tibetans.[5] But this continuum cannot withstand internal ruptures, the alienation of communities from their own historical past, as Temsula Ao writes in her "Prayer of a Monolith", "They dislodged me from my mooring / They tore me from her side / They chipped and chiseled / They gave me altered dimensions".[6] The unrepresentable trace arises in death and disjunction from a lived past, but it arises in the present as an experience of 'thrownness'. The meaning of life emerges from such epiphany-filled moments of opposition between 'imaginary' and 'real' and the members of the tribe relate this opposition to a desire for expanding the world. This can be exemplified in the oppositional role of 'male' and 'female' among the Abo-Tani group of people. The function of men is to face 'outside' in the form of encountering the other in war, trade and exchange, while the function of women lies in protecting the space of the community. Defense is against the outside dangers by enclosing the community space. The Abo-Tani people perform the rite of controlling the war-trophy and after the rite is over they burn it and bury it under a big stone and pronounce, "Go to your place, we send to you under the ground, we close the door of the earth (...) Till ten generations you will not be able to hurt our descendents (...)".[7] In other words, there is an opening before the closure and anthropologically, it is meant for self-defense. What needs to be investigated is how this picture of self-other relationship is now transformed into a dialogic possibility. The paper can address this in terms of experiential narratives from generic tribes and locate how such narratives find their local ramifications. *Who now becomes an Other and whether the identity of the Other is determined only in an act of response or in a co-sharing of a continuum needs to be investigated.* One can also inquire whether the imaginary continuum of a shared and lived space involves reciprocal recognition. The question can be deepened by asking what ontological barriers are created by an asymmetric federal State that localizes and pluralizes tribes in order to constitute the periphery. *How does one break through this logic of centre-periphery relations?*

Methodological Musings

At the methodological level, one has to remember that the binary opposition and reciprocity of self-other relationship manifested in experiential narratives finds its textual correlate in the form of displacement and substitution of a signifier by another. Such a displacement of signifiers is experientially grounded in the embedded character of a 'form of life' in language, as if language is structured as experience, which in turn, gives a linguistic structure to language. Most of the conceptual and narrative elements of language are experiential and the content of such an experiential language is supplied by a 'form of life' that supplies 'content' to both language and life as such.

Anthropological sciences as 'bricolage'[8] function to explain the 'natural' cr the 'concrete', although they are designed to explain things specific to human cultures. For example, totem as a marker of 'differentiation' belonging to a culture explains a fact that is 'natural' or 'biological' but its significance lies in the realm of culture in terms of meanings. *When human beings as agents could see themselves as an extension of nature outside, they further evolved a linguistically mediated rational order that established a unity between 'nature' and 'culture'.* Similarly any anthropological concept that is invoked in understanding and interpreting a form of life originates from the natural world, but derives its meaning from the world of culture. This derived meaning acts as bricolage as it serves the purpose of explaining the natural phenomenon in cultural terms, which is more cultural than instrumental. *What is culturally important for meanings is that they are liable to be transmuted from one kind of meaning into another within a body of linguistically coded myths and narratives.* Meanings, therefore, serve as bricolage themselves, as they often act as metaphor, analogy or perform some other functional roles. Such roles are performed in terms of transformation of some elements of myths or narratives into some other meanings and such transformations are guided by an anthropological reason of serving a purpose of nature that enacts a cultural and social role as well.

Language acts as a bricolage of signs[9], which are made to do other things than were originally intended, that is, to represent things or objects named within a culture. On the one hand such names could become 'conceptual tools' for analysis of cultures and on the other, they can serve as signs meant for serving purposes other than they were intended purporting 'transformations'. But this anthropological search for a system of concepts or rather some kind of universals is perpetually destabilized by the empirical possibility of difference as it obtains in a variety of cultures occupying different mental universes demonstrating a kind of compatibility/incompatibility between signs. Inter-relationship between signs as a cultural fact or norm brings us to the point that coincidence between signs in terms of compatibility of meanings is merely engineered and it is a kind of engineering. But no amount of engineering can make 'signs'; the means of representations coincide with its 'end', the meaning, to make sign self-identical or something that is present to itself. Rather signs as means of representation would lead to other signs with a kind of discontinuity between themselves, which can take the form of substitution and displacement, instead of a systematic difference of particular meanings.[10] The difference is instituted in the form of a rupture in the relationship between the signifier and the signified as it is conceived within language in the form of a binary opposition or reciprocity. Both the signifier and the signified arise in a field of freeplay of signs not pre-determined by given anthropological difference. It is the trace of this difference in empirical details that semantically makes difference between signs true within a field of infinite substitutions in the 'closure' of a finite discourse of anthropology. Such a freeplay within the field of anthropology does not allow the field to be completely determined by a prior theory of knowledge, but rather keeps it open to interpretations, which is an infinite possibility of freeplay.

Critiquing Anthropology

The moment of freeplay in anthropology is conceptualized by a radical deconstruction of field into texts and vice-versa. This also marks an overlapping between the anthropological and the philosophical, meaning a strategic location of language within the discourse of epistemology and political economy. Earlier forms of ethnographic representations in terms of decoding of natural into cultural now assume a more complex institutional form of power that anthropological discourses attempts to rationalize. For example, the notion of 'writing machine'[11] as advanced by George Marcus that qualifies shifts in anthropological praxis from describing the richness of human culture in an ingenious way to participation in an already existing and contestatory world of representation. This is a kind of anthropology that reflects on its heteronymous origins: questions that are raised from point of views of cultural dominance, identity clashes and political conflicts, which are not just embedded in representations, but introduce a new politics of interpretation of the candidate's social facts by re-orienting the usual contexts of meaning. Such heteronymous anthropology changes the very notion of embedding by following a challenging strategy of structural analysis with an emphasis on agency roles that emerge from the long term trends of history.[12] This mode of anthropology re-embeds its usual conceptual tools drawn from ethnography not just in a form of life, but moves beyond by way of altering the subjects of observation and interpretation. The question is how the subjects of ethnographic observation are changed? First by refusing to assign them a 'given' place within their own societies, where the given is identified to either confirm or revise the already arrived at anthropological notion or theory about a particular society. Next, by substituting the relation by which the native informant representing the essence of society's organizing principles of identity and difference becomes the 'signifier' of anthropological discourse by a 'heterology'. To borrow Georges Bataille's definition of heterology, one might surmise,

> ...heterology is opposed to any homogeneous representation of the world, in other words, to any philosophical system.[13]

The change in the status of the subject could now be understood from radical difference between an interpreter's identification of the native within her cultural habitus or form of life and the constitutive gap that exists between such a form of life and the heterogeneous forces of giving an identity to the form of life. One example could be drawn from the divergence between Europe's imperializing moves of discovering an America by assimilating it in their own terms and Ameri-Indian's self-description of being 'Indigene'. Such divergence could also be conceptualized in terms of an imperial politics of 'seeing the world as the other sees it' or in terms of a knowable other, who is deprived of exteriority and alterity. This is constituting an other with a constitutive gap between 'the way the other sees the world' and the interpreter's appropriation of that world in a 'god's eye point of view'. In heteronymous anthropology's search for new meanings by overcoming the constitutive aporia between the imposed otherhood and the constitution of the self of the native, what is posited is an alternative to future driven goals of disciplines of history and anthropology. This jibes well with undermining the linear historical progress from colony to post-colony to global that throws out the native only as a 'proper name' to give rise to an alternative to any pre-existing structure of representation. Such an alternative would not merely be supplemental to what the pre-existing ones lacked, nor would it be an absolute a priori consisting of all the means of access to the other including logico-linguistic embeddedness, but an open substitute 'outside the subject' or better called as one who comes after the subject.[14] This is a subject with irreducible difference, a subject without alterity. Does anthropology's interface with philosophy attempt to reduce this alterity to a set of fixed norms, values and rules as embedded in language, which Wittgenstein conceived to be a 'form of life'? In other words, reduction of difference to sameness by way of bringing the other within a rule-centric linguistic description is a strategy of adopting an intersubjectivity based shared understanding of the other that gives rise to an anti-ethnocentrism, modernity's 'empty signifier' for self-validating and self-justifying critique. This calls for an inquiry into the question, if ethnography is embedded in linguistic conventions of meaning and interpretation following a rule, how does one account for practices of a community that are not grounded in those specific rules that do not as yet form a part of Anthropological-Philosophical discourse?

Mapping an Ethnophilosophical Culture of Northeast India: From an Ethnophilosophical angle, one question that arises at this point is the linguistic embeddedness of participation of nature-as-subject in the constitution of the life-world. In the narrative constitution of the life-world as a Thou (in the second person form), wisdom stands out as an irreducible quality of that life-world. Narrative, in the first person mode gives rise to the 'hard problem' of making intentional acts of any constitutive subjectivity converge with the horizon of meaning already formed within the life-world.

This 'hard problem' gets dissolved in the participative mode of subjectivity that constitutes itself in terms of an inalienable relationship with a co-subject, be it nature, stone or animal. This is the second person subjectivity always simultaneously apparent and real, immanent and transcendent, genetic and specific that is always co-constituted from the point of view of what it has always already constituted. It is no interpellation determined by mutually participating poles of subjectivity that simultaneously shows a fissure and a fusion, nor it is non-participation of a priori conceptual and logical forms, but a co-reductive occasion of wisdom. This is in contrast to first or third person narratives that separate life-world from experiences of life. In the second person mode of narrative, a fundamental lack in the constitution of subjectivity never appears to be the driving force to narrativize or enact the self and the 'center' of the narrative. Co-reductivity of the self and nature again is not something that the whole legacy of linguistic philosophy's therapeutic judgments are wary of, namely, how our intelligence is already dazzled by deceptive uses of language. Further co-reductivity of self and nature is not the Kantian and Husserlian canonical notion of transcendental and anti-psychologistic move of prioritizing categories of understanding or consciousness as the ground for world making, which justifies our natural feeling that by means of these we have "caught reality in our net". One can further say that the view about co-reductivity of self and nature does not envisage a dichotomy between them, but introduces a diachrony of constituting each other in a space of interrelationship, which is neither an external standpoint nor a 'brain in a vat' kind of situation. It rather cures slowly the habit of therapeutic philosophy's analysis of linguistic embeddedness of reason by a kind of non-projection of how language constitutes itself in the realm of inter-relationship, without which it becomes a language without a horizon of the world. From this point of view, language and world are mutually reducible in a constitutive sense and not in a genetic sense, as there is neither a transcendental point of view nor a naturalistic explanation already there in language. Therefore, the subjectivity of Khasis constitute a life-world only to get constituted by it, not carefully constructed in narrative synthesis between self and nature.

(a) **Khasis**: The Khasi term for thirty phrase as "Laiphew jait" is conceived to be not just a representation of the number 30, but is conceived to be meaning 'all types'. For example, 'laiphew syiem" means many kings; "laiphew mrad" means many animals. Philosophically speaking the Khasi concept of all and many as a generic concept is simultaneously particular and general. Concept of numbers to instantiate all or many are place markers within the structure of all or many, which is simultaneously predicative and impredicative. Following Berry's paradox[15] in mathematics, one could say that the if one names 'a number more than thirty', one can do it with the generic, but if one names a number less than thirty, one can do it with a specific name. The application of the concept of all or many would apply only as indeterminate count, while Laiphew or thirty as a definite number would apply to these indeterminate categories of all or many. There is a fuzzying of the particular and the generic, but either of them could be applied within the structure of counting. In other words, the reference of all or many cannot be determined by the sense of Laiphew or conversely the sense of Laiphew cannot be determined by the rigid designator thirty. Khasi ethnographer Barnes L. Mawrie provides us a further information about Laiphew, by calling it a 'perfect number' that stands for 'all or everything'. How the Khasis construct this recognitional capacity is represented by a narrative on old dances of Khasis reconstructed by Barnes L. Mawrie.

In many cultures all over the world, dances have originated from man's imitation of the movements of animals and birds. Among the Khasis too, many dances have originated in this way. The Khasis of old speak of 'ka shad ki laiphew mrad' (dance of thirty animals, meaning all animals). In the golden era, when it is believed that man and animals spoke the same language, the animals shared many activities of man. Thus there were business transactions even among animals known as Ka Iew Luri Lura (market of chaos). Then there was the periodic universal dance called 'ka shad ki laiphew mrad' wherein every kind of animal and bird came in their best costumes to show their solidarity by participating in this dance.[16]

The idea of perfect number is an ideal type that names everything, apparently the type is without extension, but surely it is the mark of the recognitional capacity of the subject by which the subject picks out things that fit the ideal type in the world.[17] Animals in this narrative are imagined as the lawgivers, who are imitated in the human world. Animal dances serve as the bricolage to explain human dances and their contexts (such as form and situation of performance) act as the medium for transmission of natural into cultural. The narrative assumes three stages of development: first the dance of all the animals serving as the structureless domain of all possible forms of dance; second, the emergence of shared meanings of life in the ordinary cacophony of life, called as 'chaos' marking the birth of a shareable language; third, solidarity between animals and birds signifying the unifying dimensions of dance that happens across a variety of species. The three stages taken together are itself a mix of a variety of purposes and functions that are open to human interpretations, as all these go into formation of a shareable code of dance and language in human beings. Dance, in a sense, is giving a way to language and it lies in an in-between domain between dance and language, between animals, birds and humans. If we take this to be a transition from dance to language and language to dance this transition is given life in the narrative imagination. Further, dance itself breaks the linguistic barrier that is apparently there between humans and animals. Dance simultaneously creates a kind of dissensus between two different species and it also creates a sense of sharing the space, or rather sharing a sense of communality. This imagination is a necessity, as mere linguistic representation of a practice would not retain the pre-linguistic contact with other beings and the sense of responsibility towards them. In the very idea of dance, both the difference with the other and the infinite capacity of ceaseless natural events to arouse phrases that 'dance' in order to give language a sense of what is other to one's own being. This is a dance of expressing solidarity and dependence between animal and human worlds, which lies outside the enclosed space of linguistic meaning. Such a dance establishes "the law of the house, the initial organization of a dwelling space"[18] that also brings out the underside of human languages that represses what is cognitively shared between humans and non-human beings.

Nature, as it gets related to the human subject within Khasi culture turns it into a co-intentional subject which can exist without representation within the phenomenon. In other words there is no self-conscious imposition of forms on Nature apart from human-nature relationship, which embeds all other forms that could be given to Nature through tales, narratives and arts. This embedding of inseparable relationship between humans and Nature gives rise to the wisdom of Khasi life-world, which relates the anthropological categories of self-understanding to the particular life-world experiences. Narratives, as in the first person mode, are not merely unifying structures of stories that give cohesiveness to life, but they embed the inseparable second person relationship that gives rise to co-subjectivity between the first and the second person in the very world of Khasis. Such subjective and objective grounds of reason, which set up an embedded interrelatedness between the self and the world express themselves in the historicity of participation of objects of nature in that domain of culture and linguistic meaning , constituting Khasi life-world.

(b) **Apatanis**: As descendents of primal couple Abo and Tani, Apatanis can be treated as the representative tribal group in Arunachal Pradesh who still carry on their tradition by way of participation in the era of modernity and change. The paper can inquire into several such features of Apatani life-world that finds their expression in their wisdom of artifactuality. The so-called 'representation of tradition' in anthropology assumes a language of self-presence, which is manifest in an experience that produces its own time and space. Also the unifying, self-consistent and self-justifying idea of a tradition arises out of the concept of representation in anthropology. This strategy of interpreting by way of representation, as practiced in anthropology bases itself on the categories of understanding that are derived from observations of a tradition. It is in this sense that tradition arises after the act of representation and it does not precede representation.

Crucial epistemological questions arise here, whether this precedence of representation makes possible an internal realism about their belief while making it open to an externalist interpretation. My attempt here is to recuperate the lost subject in their own narrative that accesses their world. These are descriptions about the world that fit their linguistically embedded world to provide them access to that world that further instantiates for the whole set of anthropologists and ethnographers the 'reality' of their world. But this world is discrete, non-relational that only provides a disengaged and non-universal generality of constitution of the subject. Although the ethnographic-anthropological bias lies in a juridical autonomy to construct their discursive subjects, as if such subjects are constituted by and in rules guiding their practices; such subjects remain open to deconstruction of their assumed stability, rather they do not represent the truth of their lives by presenting them as mere candidates in a story of life.

Critically conceived in this manner, meanings assigned to artifacts, ornaments, tattoos etc. do not 'represent' a content, but stand as identity markers that act as candidate conditions of representation. What anthropologists can do is to examine to what extent such markers are specific to a culture. In examining this, they turn to conceptual understanding of these markers as it obtains within the tribe under study and attempt to establish some kind of logical and meaningful connection between one and the other tribe. The idea of uniqueness, therefore, turns out to be another conceptual product in anthropologists explanations. In case of a tribe like Apatani, a native scholar interprets the identity markers as follows:

> The tattooing of their lower chin, hair knot with skew on forehead, belting of loin cloth with dyed cane work hanging from their waist, putting on cane woven ring on

> the hinge etc. are the men folk of the Apatanis. The tattooing on their forehead to the tip of the nose and lower chin, wearing of British type skirt and jacket, wearing of blue beads and necklace, ear-ring etc. are the womenfolk. Both folks are characteristic of the tribe's identity and beauty, but more importantly of the cultural and religious traits of the tribe.[19]

The scholar seems to be emphasizing the uniqueness of cultural and religious traits of the Apatanis as reflected in their dress code, mostly described by him in terms of artifacts and ornaments. These artifacts and ornaments give meanings in terms of cultural and religious traits that are not merely representational of the identity and beauty, but express matters of faith and aesthetics. These expressions cannot be understood from the representational affect, but they should be diachronically linked up with the statements of belief such as, "Miyu saling La Gyunyang Santa Tiggo Santa Lingi Du"(Men is born with the religious rites and ceremonies and therefore, we can't live a prosperous life without the ceremony of rites and duties.) These statements of belief are correlated with artifacts. But this correlation is something internal to the community. Takhe Kani provides a catalogue of such diachronic correlations in the case of costumes of the Apatani priest,

1. Zillang: It is a piece of outer robe of the priest, which is used in ceremonies of Myoko, Murung, Subu only. It is highly designed on the body and borderline and is in technique of Zillang Laying (fret shape), Abyopro (a geometrical pattern), Laying Pinchu (fret shape), Khiibolarko (cross hatching), Nessuarko (cross-bold), Karnii (loop coil), Obyatunii(zigzag), Pesuuhidda (Horring bone) and other designs (...). The colour and designs are the choice of the weaver. Usually colour combination of this robe is Nuhu (red), Pyallang (light red), Nupu (white), Tiipya (black-blue), Pyami (light-yellow). The priest and the layman cannot use them in other days.
2. Zibo: This type of outer robe is used only by Bulyang or village council, who leads the community feast demonstration of Myoko known as Khiibo Gyonii during its ceremony. The colour combination is same as Zilang but designs are more

simple than that of Zilang. This is not used by the priest.[20]

What emerges from this description of the design, function and the use of clothes is a complex weaving of belief and the design on the body of the wearer, who is a priest or leader of the village council. The relationship between designs and their function in a ceremony is not articulated in terms of specific meanings for certain purposes. The meaning remains only functional, understood in terms of ritual roles or social roles that such meanings correlate with. Without the usual linguistic concept of meaning, the correlations through which the meaning is established gives rise to a different notion of embedding. Meanings get embedded through artifacts in occasions and contexts that link up artifacts and social roles that call for the use of such artifacts. Each of these artifacts present something like a matrix of meaning, the elements of which are constituted by rich textures of designs, colours and shapes that are produced within the culture. The matrix of meaning that arises out of a presuppositionless relationship between what is humanely created in the form of artifacts and the realm of human meaning that is linguistic can be a field of study on its own. The paper can contextualize the inquiry into the complexity of the relationship between belief and design to bring out the artifacuality of Apatani wisdom.

Ethnography in a Representational Mode

Western canons of ethnography as practiced in Northeast India turns their vision on the subject society in terms of abstractions and place those abstractions upon the society under study. One example would make the canonization clear. An interesting observation made by J.P. Mills on Ao Nagas talks about a belief among the Christian as well as non-Christian Ao's about striking down a tree on a cultivated land, which is that the field must be purified with an offering of an egg, six pieces of chicken and six pieces of dried meat. This explanation of a belief gets canonized in the form of religion, or better, it gets religion-ized in such an act of representation.[21]

J. P. Mills's extraordinarily supple description of Ao Naga culture provides a textual entry into the symbolic realm of the

Ao Naga mind. The 'text' needs to be reconfigured and re-read by establishing the intricate links in its surface representation. The spheres of Ao Naga life are demarcated from the given configuration of the text, and one could try to separate the 'private' and the 'public' spheres of Ao Naga life even though such markers are not readily available. What Mills names as 'domestic' could possibly provide a basis for wider arenas of life by streamlining the values, practices and habits of the domestic sphere. Conversely, the domestic sphere can become a sustainable ground for continuance of the practices in 'public' life. Even without strictly demarcated spheres of 'private' and 'public', Mills' preferred coinages, such as domestic and other spheres, and arrange the text in such a manner that it envelopes distinct spheres of life. We propose a reading of the Ao Naga domestic realm as described by Mills in order to experience the sphere of domesticity as the microcosm of intricate linkages of various symbols that also sustain practices in wider spheres, giving rise to their specific domesticity.

Following such ethnographic interventions, the paper can inquire into what constitutes the sphere of domestic in the Ao Naga life? We designate two levels: *(i)* the material cultural resources; and *(ii)* the representational types available in language. We take these two levels of constitution of the domestic not because they erect the limits of a designated sphere but because they provide a route from the 'concrete' to the 'formal', the specific transition to cognizable 'forms' that stand as the finished products of their 'domestic' realm. Further, the specific transition from one level to another bears the process of linguistic appropriation of their life-experiences that sets their horizon. Mills' textualization of their horizon provides an exploratory poetics of their lives, the meanings of which need to be disseminated. For example, the village as a place of inhabitation is surrounded by a belt of bamboo clumps and light jungle. The name of the village represents a spatial feature: 'Changtongia' derives its 'root' from a kind of thin bamboo called chuchuo.[22] In a way the name of the village and its surroundings get identified, and the name acquires its ostensible reference. But the demarcation of the village paths by fine spear-oaks brought during the present villagers' migration retraces their long forlorn footprints in the well-ordered plantation of these trees. One can read an ecological balancing among a chosen place of habitation, the natural surroundings, and the planned arrangements, all synchronized within a village, remaining as a simultaneous marker of such a creation in the act of naming. Interestingly, a village name such as 'Yongyimsen' recalls the memory of long-departed Konyak settlers with its new connotation as 'new village of the Yong people'. The Ao Naga way of naming reveals a synchrony between the present and the past.

Naming suffices the fundamental purpose of the binding together the settlers of the village and it spills over onto certain organized functions. The 'defence' of the village is secured by making 'fences': 'The fence, which was of wooden stakes, lashed together and bristling with *panjis*, stretched right around the village."[23] Such fences are necessary for the safety of the village and are marked in a festival called Atsutsu Kimak or Urang Kimak. There is a strategic planting of long creepers whose tendrils are trained down the bamboo, which are used to thwart enemies. Such defence strategy links up defence with certain beliefs and norms, norms such as the participation of the community in making fences and the belief of growing creepers. What is revealing here is the continuation of the practice of growing creepers as a custom, because its discontinuation would weaken defence, thereby many plants are preserved that would otherwise have become extinct. How does the preparation for defence become a domestic affair? Firstly, by the participation of the community in the erection of the fences, and, secondly, the day becomes one of celebration as every young male participant visits the dormitories of the girls and are offered rice beer, which converts it to a 'domestic' occasion.

The observance of community works and customs related to it is obligatory. Even the growing of certain plants serves the double function of defending the community as well as being a symbolic ratification of defence plans. Moreover such symbolic and customary observances performed as a part of a common goal partially constitutes the realm of the domestic, while an act of celebration of the real work through reception and festivity adds the 'intent' to the symbolic. A symbolic performance without its celebrating mode does not acquire a decipherable meaning in the domestic sphere of Ao Nagas. Therefore, the domestic is in no way limited to a piecemeal symbolic act of the individual; unless it is opened up to a collective celebration of a work meant to serve the common purpose it is never completed.

This aspect of the refinement of task and aesthetic sense operates at the level of pleasure and satisfaction among the Ao Nagas. Later every *khel* owned a drum. Let us reflect on Mills's elaborate description of the drums:

> They consist of huge logs, slit along one side and partially hollowed out. One end is carved to represent what is undoubtedly a buffalo's head, with horns lying back along the drum . . . The tongue of the buffalo often protrudes and turns up against the upper lip, and, as if to personify the drum still further, a human face is often carved on the tongue.[24]

This description of the drums and the personified motifs on it signify purposive social and cultural performances. At the level of representation, these drums and the motifs closely relate to the domestic moorings of the Ao Naga life. The paper can further look into the ideas of domesticity in Ao Naga life and whether such an idea has its connection with the larger world.

The Construction of Narrative Self: Angami Naga Meanings

J.H. Hutton's remarkable work on the Angami Nagas discusses what he termed as Angami Naga superstitions. He describes these as:

> The Angamis belief that whoever approaches the foot of the rainbow will die is explained by saying that the spirit of the rainbow will kill the person, but no reason is given for the belief that it is dangerous to plant hedges of 'cactus' (i.e. *Euphorbia antiquorum)* because they cause storms, or for the belief that a man's stomach aches when someone at a distance is molesting his property.[25]

What is interesting is the narrative that link up a statement of belief with another belief. The explanation given for the cause of death by touching the foot of rainbow is the work of the spirit residing in the rainbow. This interpretation gives primacy to the concept of the rainbow spirit that enacts the death, and another line of interpretation could be a narrative reconfiguration of the sight of rainbow that suggests that the colour bands of a rainbow manifest a spirit. However, such an explanation does not have an expected consistency and hence appears like superstition to an observer. Belief represents a narrative and fictional nature in which narrative becomes the medium to link up disparate phenomena and entities. The notion of the 'spirit' in the rainbow is invoked to explain the death caused by touching the foot of the rainbow. Again, the 'foot of a rainbow' is an imagined construction to signify its declining semi-circular arch, a visual illusion or spectre that gives rise to such narrative construction. It obviously lacks the usual narrative elements such as rhetoric or trope but bears an important characteristic of the narrative by presenting an explanation that leaves an inexplicable that has to be accommodated by belief. In the same extract, the cause of stomach pain as someone else molesting one's property presents a metaphorical picture of one's mutual loss, which can be best described in terms of a physiological attack corresponding to the act of ransacking of one's property. Two kinds of explanations can also be traced. In the first belief, the visual representation gives rise to a strategy of containment, and in the second, causal correspondence between 'pain' and 'molestation' established through an analogous equivalence represents a belief about natural causation. How do these explanations acquire the status of belief?

Given this introduction to the nature of Angami Naga belief, one can try to see the play of such belief in the narrative construction of its genealogy. This would provide a basis for narrative construction of experiential notion of self.

Anthropocentrism in Defining an Agency

Such ethnographic constructions of self-identity through tales and narratives basically aim at creating a world for themselves within which not only their beliefs would find a place but they would also construct a place of dwelling. Such a place of dwelling is not guided by rules of social formations or other such abstract rules in operation rather it gives rise to an anteriority that disengages itself from reasons and beliefs. This is the place of wisdom and it can transcend the borderlines of reason. Wisdom, further, creates the possibility of conceiving the material well-being of societies in terms of reliability of sharing cultural life and therefore opens up a greater possibility of freedom that is otherwise curtailed by anthropology's blank assumption of material progress as the key to development of societies. On a theoretical plank, wisdom discloses itself only when the borders drawn by conventional reason between language and world is blurred by different beliefs and their practices. Beliefs, in other words, remain the mainstay of indigenous and native societies of northeast India. Beliefs also signify various ways of constructing the world in language and this becomes possible only when beliefs start disclosing in concrete historical and cultural terms. This further produces a cognitive inclusion of belief within the world that is made by those beliefs themselves and this is possible by including language within the world as a medium of communication and representation. Such an inclusivity, definitely, does not in any way blur our capabilities of making distinctions, rather multiply such distinction by an act of inclusion.

Such a process of inclusions and demarcation marks the growth of a proper classification—is it possible to move from 'abstract' linguistic classifications' to 'ritual classifications'? From there on, can one bring out in formulaic terms the embedded 'forms of life' that such classifications represent? To what extent a scheme of classification influences the 'subjectivity' of a self-presenting identity?

Anthropology only narrates how such inclusions/exclusions are achieved in a certain mode of cultural practice or, more generally, in a certain society. The moment such a story of inclusion and world making is read from a perspective that is anterior to a culture of reason, there is a disengagement from the contents of what is only included and one *looks for an external reality* that would possibly justify such inclusions. In the context of Northeast tribes, performance of war-rituals that included the act of feeding the spirits of dead and enemy-spirits as well constitutes an 'external reality' for justifying the war preparedness of a village community. Remembrances of such preparedness talks of the enemy as the 'other' while they are symbolically included within the social rituals of a community.

But one cannot externalist the whole way, as one's perspective already lies within some anterior world-view, embedded within a form of life and therefore refuses to be closed onto the same and engages itself with the other. A level of well-defined vantage that could be transcendental and inter-subjective could back such understanding and knowing of the other. How anthropology's 'artifactual objects' of knowledge deal with such philosophical backup has been the residual aspect of theory building in anthropology, the primary, nonetheless, describing how a particular society achieves this level of self-understanding.

The idea of the artifactuality here takes the form of a law of sociality without specifying the gift of exchange, but it only specifies the ritual well-being of the community. In doing so, the parables and hymns of belief acquire a kind of authenticity that spills into a larger realm of meaning of life than mere linguistic embeddedness of meanings. For example, a strange illness believed to be induced by ancestral spirits, called Iigii-Lirung among the Apatanis is believed to be incurable by modern medicine, as it is a sickness of the soul. Therefore the cure comes from praying to ancestors and by offering them sacrifices. The whole conception of illness in terms of sickness of the soul is not merely bodily one, but it is supposed to be curable only by way of rituals that modern doctors cannot perform. This emphasizes the healing role of the priests, thereby meaning the presence of ancestors in somebody's present life. Also this has a deeper meaning dimension: it is not like a bodily cut, but an affect of the supernatural. This calls for special sacrifices such as sacrifice of castrated boar, which requires very special ways of performing the same. One sees here an act of drawing of a harmony between meanings, artifacts, rituals and other aspects of Apatani life that is made possible only by an exercise of beliefs and associated reasons with it. Part of the domain of belief also remains 'inarticulate', as there are no sufficient reasons that can fully explain the wisdom aspect of beliefs. In a similar vein the Khasi notion of Ka Rngiew considered as innate personhood is embedded in the belief of being a human.

Can we also extend the argument by positing that the inarticulate aspects of cultures are those that cannot be brought within linguistic articulation because of the 'limited' character of human language and therefore the articulate aspects of a culture emanate from those deeper inarticulate features and aspects that remain embedded within the culture? Here one moves beyond the realm of reason and tries to discover something that has not been properly articulated within the culture, yet without which the culture cannot be fully articulated. So the moot question is, can any culture ever articulate something that is intrinsically inarticulate and that which is part of its wisdom?

In Lieu of a Conclusion

The dialectic between the 'inarticulate' and 'articulate' is concretized in a few foundational binary oppositions such as native and nation, civic and ethnic, underground and overground, and so on. Such oppositions are sustained by a structure of correspondence between the self and the Other without presenting a possibility of transformation. As an example of embeddedness of such a dialectic, one could locate in the language (*i*) the pre-ontic murmur, (*ii*) prior contact with the Other, and (*iii*) transformation of the natural world in interpretative uses of language. But such a combined functioning of what we call embeddedness in language is based on the condition of operation of practices, in terms of how language accesses these practices. Access to these practices does not happen as something prior to language that lies out there in the world but as an available representation of a concept, which is accessed in language to exhibit the original intentional experiences that present the referent instantiating the concept. This assumes the knowledge of conditions of assertibility by which the application of a concept would either be true or false. Such knowledge occurs in the specific context of a community that anthropologists establish through an intuitive knowledge of the Other. The radical alterity of the Other, which is the subject without alterity, appears with differentiating, non-relational and non-universal generality that produces discrete notions and concepts within culture, the value of which is contingent and undecidable. Embeddedness within language as a global notion becomes effective here without decidable and determinable value content, which makes the anthropologists' ascription of 'Otherness' possible.

It is this ascribed Otherness, from the point of view of ethnography's bare particulars, to a Khasi or an Apatani that a simultaneous assumption of stability of the subject in language and iterability of subject of language is constituted. The ethnographic-anthropological bias lies in a juridical autonomy to construct their discursive subjects, as if such subjects are constituted by and in rules guiding their practices. Such subjects remain open to deconstruction of their assumed stability; rather they do not represent the truth of their lives by presenting them as mere candidates in a story of life. In case of assertion by smaller ethnic identities, it is not just repositioning themselves as ethnic elites, but it is also re-articulation against the dominant. Moving beyond affiliation, it sets a domain of articulation, a way to meet demands of democratization. Those who lose their non-representative power see it as an attempt of the 'Others' to reposition them. Therefore, they respond from a carefully designed strategy of ensuring their own power. The fear is that, if once given in, there will be other such occasions of those who had hitherto remained away from such assertions raising their voices. There is an expressed helplessness on such occasions from the rulers that be. It is at this moment that re-invoking old faultlines is blended and blurred by new alignments and break-offs become a strategy of maintaining a potentially collapsing ideological hegemony.

In other words, clamour against political and economic inequality could be ideologically suppressed by the dominant and this is what acts as the counterproductive mechanism in disarticulating the very peace process that is initiated in a given situation. Apart from such 'peace regime' types, the knowledge of peace assumes a distinct historical and cultural form. The knowledge is constituted phenomenologically by way of bracketing the non-textual connections with ground reality, which almost borders on an unrecognized ethnography of peoples of the region. Knowledge from such an ethnographic context holds the secrets of many an ethnic conflict, which epistemic-anthropological regimes overlook.

NOTES AND REFERENCES

1. I have adopted this argument from Arjun Appadurai's statement that global cultural flow occurs through several disjunctures, such as disjunctures between ethnoscapes, technoscapes, mediascapes and ideoscapes. See, Arjun Appadurai, "Disjuncture and Difference in Global Cultural Economy" in Simon During (ed.), *The Cultural Studies Reader*, 3rd edition, Routledge, London and New York, 2007, pp. 216-26.
2. Ernesto Laclau, *Emancipations*, Verso, London, 1996, pp. 53-4.
3. I borrow this argument from Jacques Derrida, *Parages, Galilie*, Paris, 1986, p. 66.
4. Mamang Dai, *The Legends of Pensam*, Penguin Papers India, New Delhi, 2006, p. 71.
5. H.E. Kauffman, "The Thread-Square Symbol of Nagas of Assam" in *The Journal of the Royal Anthropological Society*, vol. 73, no. 1/2, 1943, p. 104
6. Temsula Ao, *Songs from Here and There*, NEHU Publications, Shillong, 2003, p. 4
7. C. Von Furer-Haimendorf, *The Apa Tani & their Neighbours*, Routledge, London, pp. 165-6.
8. Claude Levi Strauss, The Savage Mind, trans. John and Doreen Weightman, Chicago University Press, Chicago, 1966, pp. 16-7.
9. Jacques Derrida, "Structure, Sign, and Play in the Human Sciences", in *The Structuralist Controversy: The Languages of Criticism and the Sciences of Man*, ed. by Richard Macksey and Eugenio Donato, Johns Hopkins University Press, Baltimore, 1970, pp. 247-72.

10. Jacques Derrida, *Spurs: Nietzsche's Styles*, trans. Barbara Harlow, University of Chicago Press, Chicago, p. 117.

11. George E. Marcus, *Critical Anthropology Now: Unexpected Contexts*, Shifting Constituencies and Changing Agendas, School of American Research Press, Santa Fe, 1999, pp. 7-9.

12. Donald L. Donham, *History, Power, Ideology: Central Issues in Marxism and Anthropolgy*, 2nd edition University of California Press, Berkeley, 1999, pp. 56-7.

13. Quoted in Franson Manjali, *Literature and Infinity*, Indian Institute of Advanced Study, Shimla, 2001, p.39,n.14.

14. Jacques Derrida, *Sur Parole: Instantanés philosophiques*, Aube, Paris, 1999, p. 63.

15. Mr.G. Berry, the librarian of Oxford University invented a paradox, first reported by Bertrand Russell in 1908. It goes like this, if by definition, there is an integer which is "the smallest positive integer not nameable in less than thirty syllables" is an integer nameable in only eleven syllables as quoted in the definition, but that is not nameable by definition. The definition defines the smallest positive integer, but tells us that it is not definable in the exact number of syllables in which it defines the number in the very definition. This is a paradox of self-referentiality embedded in any language, a 'form of life'. In the Khasi context, Laiphew gives rise to a similar paradox: where the description Laiphew does not fit with the meaning of Laiphew as defined in counting natural numbers. For details, Russell, B., "Mathematical Logic is Based on the Theory of Types", *Am. J. of Mathematics 30*, 1908, p. 223.

16. Barnes L. Mawrie, SDB, *The Khasis and Their Natural Environment: A Study of the Eco-consciousness and Eco-spirituality of the Khasis*, Vendrame Institute of Publications, Shillong, 2001, p. 110, n. 9.

17. Gareth Evans, *The Varieties of Reference*, Oxford University Press, Oxford, 1982, pp.227-28.

18. Jacques Derrida, *Writing and Difference*, trans. Alan Bass, University of Chicago Press, Chicago, 1978, pp. 169-192.

19. Takhe Kani, *Socio-Religious Ceremonies of the Apatanis of Arunachal Pradesh*, Frontier Publishers and Distributors, Itanagar, 1st edition, 1996, pp. 4-5.

20. *Ibid.*, pp. 28-9.
21. J.P. Mills, *The Ao Nagas*, Directorate of Art and Culture, Govt. of Nagaland, Kohima, rpt., 2003,pp.305-6.
22. *Ibid.*, p.72.
23. *Ibid.*, p.73.
24. *Ibid.*, pp.76-7.
25. J. H. Hutton, *The Angami Nagas*, Macmillan and Co. Limited, London,1921,p. 251.

12

Making Sense of the Present through Sanu Lama's *Mṛgatṛṣṇa*

Pravesh G. Jung

The arena of philosophy in the broadest sense of the term is the term marked commons. Any intellect can graze on it and though philosophers can rightfully claim copyright to the chewed and digested fodder (that is, their respective philosophies), yet it would be a gross mistake on the part of philosophers to claim any intellectual right to the availability of the pasture itself to others. This characterization of philosophy is sufficient to both account for, as well as to justify, the *richness* or the variety of views available and displayed in the arena of philosophy (though some may preferentially label this variety as *'a mess'*). In this sense, philosophy is a public canvas available to all to appreciate, as well as to indulge in, This perhaps also explains the meta-disciplinary nature of philosophy, by virtue of which it can be used as a qualifier to any domain of inquiry. But this feature of 'open availability' of philosophy not only allows philosophy to be employed as a qualifier to qualify an intellectual inquiry rendering it as a *'philosophy of* but also opens up the possibility of' a disciplined intellectual inquiry qualifying philosophy in terms of such an inquiry itself and thereby transforming the inquiry *as philosophy'*. This paper focuses on the latter aspect and deals with philosophy as being qualified by literature with respect to our comprehension of time through the stories of Sanu Lama, The paper is thus an attempt to view a *few* short stories of Sanu Lama as a philosophical engagement with the theme of 'comprehending time'.

Grazing upon the notion of 'time' has engaged many intellects in the past and there is a rich history of this engagement. The narration of this history, though interesting, is not what this paper engages in, further, neither are metaphysical questions like 'what is time?', 'what is the nature of time? Nor are questions like 'how is time related to a narration?', or 'how is time used in a literary work?' my primary concern here. Engagement with these questions would demand that we plunge ourselves into an engagement that would befit Philosophy *of* Literature while our aim is to engage in a construction of Literature *as* Philosophy and thus my primary question would be 'what light do the stories of Sanu Lama throw upon the question of time?' The question we seek to answer, operating within the parameters of literature *as* philosophy, in relation to time, is 'how do we understand the *present*?' *We* would engage in the exposition of a possible way we comprehend time in terms of the present, within the frame of perception. and the resulting disclosed nature of this modality of comprehending time. We would then engage with the possible relation of the modality of present with the other two modalities of time, namely, the *past* and the *future* as expounded in the literary works of Sanu Lama.

To begin, one can make the observation that it is not a prerequisite for me to reflect upon *the* present to comprehend it since the present is not meaningless in itself as it presents itself to me. Indeed, to hold otherwise would lead us to an impasse. Since the moment of reflection would always follow the present that is being reflected upon it would then, no longer be the present, thereby rendering the present as impossibility. The need to reflect upon the present arises only when we intend to make this presented meaning of the present '*meaningful* in relation to *me'* or put in an effort to transform the presented present into *my present* as opposed to merely accepting the presented meaning inherent in *the present.* To this effect, reflection upon the present can thus be seen as arising out of dissatisfaction or a *lack* that I experience in the perceived present not in terms of what the present presents to me but in terms of what I intend the presented to *mean* to me. Reflection upon the present is thus an engagement with the perceived presented present to fill up this void or lack that comes along with the present that presents itself to me. Here it is essential to understand that this *appropriation* of the present is not done because the present that is presented to me is meaningless, but rather because the meaning that the present presents to me is not, so to speak, *enough* in so far as it fails to satiate me existentially. This failure of the presented present to provide within its fold an existential meaning to me can be seen as arising out of the fact that the presented present always invariably fails to encompass *me,* the *cogito,* that the present presents itself to. Thus the present though always meaningfully presented to me, fails to satiate me existentially as inherent in the meaning of the presented present is *my* very absence. The effort of rendering its meaning in *relation* to this *'I'/me* can be seen as an act of filling up this void inherent in the present. Thus the present is, of course, meaningful as presented, but it is existentially meaningful *in relation to me* only after the void has been filled. The presented meaning or the 'objective meaning' of the present must be made *existentially* meaningful in relation to my *being* in the present. This objective meaning that is inherent in the present is what leads philosophers like Merleau Ponty to hold that 'matter is 'pregnant' with its form.'[2] That is to say that if the present is to mean the totality of my perception now, then this perception, as Merleau Ponty argues,'[3] surely presents itself to me as a unity with an inherent meaning. However, if by the 'present' we are to also include what this unity means *in relation to me,* then the 'perception of the world now' or the present would demand an engagement with the present on my part. Thus in a sense, this is the impasse of the present, namely, that the present excludes *me* in its presentation of the 'objective meaning' though I am, so to speak, an indispensable part of the present as I *am* always *in* the present. Since the present is existentially comprehended by me not as the mere presented 'now' but as 'the-now-in-relation-to-me' it presupposes an engagement with the present that is presented to me. Viewed thus, the present can no longer be seen as a continuity of perceptions of the unity of all that is presented to me, but rather as the totality *of* the perception of the unity *in relation to me.* Hence, though the present is meaningful in itself, in the stories of Lama, the present that I live in and am existentially *aware* of is constituted of only those aspects of the present that I manage to relate to.

Lama in his *Yasari bitcha din,* a first person narrative, highlights this when he expresses his realization that though the 'croaks of the frog, the tadpoles in the brook, the songs of the birds, the pear tree, the neighbour's garden with fruit laden trees,' had been present all the while even after his childhood days, they had, so to speak, ceased to exist as a part of his present after his childhood days. Though they had existed as a part of the present self, they had lost their meaning in relation to him and that he had ceased to comprehend them as a part of his existentially present. Similarly, in his *Gham chaya,* though the event of Bunty's death is a fact in the present, it is an existentially meaningful part of only Paroh's (Bunty's mother) present. Bunty's death is existentially meaningful to Paroh since she relates to this fact amongst other facts presented in the present, while for the rest of existence the fact of Bunty's death is just another fact in the hordes of facts in the present.

Hence, it would be a mistake to view the continuity of time in terms of my present as a mosaic of mere continuity amongst the unity of perception. Time in terms of my present comes across as this unity of perception in their relation to me *in the now.* It is for this reason that the present is the only modality of time that can accommodate the notion of action and agency as it opens up the possibility of an activity by virtue of the void that it brings along. The act of relating *to* and *with* the presented present to make it existentially meaningful to me is what enables the very possibility of an engaged agent. I can only act in the present. After all, is it not that the realization of the present comes only in times of such engagements with what the present presents to me?

It is also this existential engagement that Lama highlights through Paroh's struggle to retain herself as an engaged agent in the world, who after having lost her son, fails to make the present meaningful to her anymore and thus feels the stagnancy of time—the feeling of being stuck in a moment. *'The park, the playground, the children playing in there, the entire surrounding'*—all of the present fails to convey any meaning to her except to force out from her the acknowledgement that they exist. Thus Paroh comes to remind herself that her engagement with the present though devoid of her son Bunty is necessary if she is to engage with the present and make any sense of time itself. She then realizes that this engagement with the present is what imparts meaning to existence itself, even if this engagement is at times a struggle, a *samgharsa*.

It is through this engagement that I comprehend *my* present as opposed to *the present* and participate in the present as an agent in the world. The notion of *the* present, is therefore, confined to the text books of the natural sciences for I live in *my* present which is in an ongoing engagement with the presented present. Thus how the present relates to me as *my* present may differ from how it relates to you giving us a spectrum of action in the same present. Lama in his *Jyoti binako ujyalo,* artistically unfolds this spectrum of possible and diverse appropriations of a fact of the presented present in terms of the blindness of seven year old Manda. Though Manda's blindness is a fact in the world, the appropriations of this fact by Dhanraj (her father), Chandra (her mother), Deepu (her brother), Dr. Wangdhi (their family doctor), and by Manda herself varies. The story highlights how each of these characters relate to the fact of Manda being blind and how they appropriate and comprehend this fact as a part of their respective presents. For Manda, it means her inability to locate her 'eyes closing' doll and thus a struggle; for her brother it means the effort that he has to make to take extra care of Manda and her feelings; for Dhanraj and Chandra, it means a life of darkness and struggle for Manda and hence in fact bringing about anxiety for them; while for Dr. Wangdhi, it means another hopeless case of lost vision bringing about a sense of his helplessness to do anything about it.

When I am *aware* of the present, it is always *my* present or the present as it relates to me that I am aware of. There is no awareness of the present in perceiving the present but its mere acceptance without awareness of this acceptance. That the 'perceptual experience' in the now or *the* present is distinct from *my* present is also evident from the fact that the former is indiscriminate in its presentation of existence to me while the latter is selective. Thus, as I am writing this paper, the present also presents to me the existence of other tables, the mats on top of those tables, my laptop, my hands, Lama's *Mṛgatṛṣṇa*, etc., but in terms of *my* present all that I am really aware of is the laptop and the book. Unlike in *the* present, where existence forces itself upon my field of reception, *my* present is selective in presenting my existence in relation to me.

But given this view of *the* present as *my* present, what is it that renders the possibility of this engagement of appropriation of the present? We could say that the present is read as *my* present by me when the present places itself in the horizon of my past or my future. It is this horizon that renders this engagement possible. But this engagement is not a process in the sense that the present is given to me and then I *impart* it an existential meaning with *reference* to my past or my future. It is not inferential in this sense. The present, though distinguishable, is not separable from the horizon in which it frames itself. In other words, *my* present is an organic whole of the horizon and the present presented to me in this horizon. It is a synthetic whole that is not synthesized in two distinct moments. I comprehend the present embedded in the horizon of my past or my future as in the very moment of comprehending the present. Appropriating what Merleau Ponty argues, though in relation to perception, one could say that one does not involve oneself in a kind of an 'intellectual synthesis' of the present with its horizon. It presents itself as a unity, as a composite whole. The possibility of filling up the void that the present brings along due to the missing 'I', is ensured by virtue of this horizon as both my past and my future necessarily include me within its fold and thus allow an entry point for the "I" in the present. My experience of the past or the future essentially must include me within their folds for it is either the *past me* in the case of the past or the *projected* me in case of the future that the *present* presents me *in the now*.

Merleau Ponty writes,

'What makes it possible for perception to be pregnant with its form is the fact that 'perception' takes place within a certain horizon.[4]

This perceptual experience gives us the passage from one

> moment to the next and thus realizes the unity of time. In this sense all consciousness is perceptual, even the consciousness of ourselves. The perceived world is always the presupposed foundation of all rationality, all value and all existence...'[5] 'Perception ... give(s) me ... presences'[6] 'perception and thought have this much in common—that both of them have a future horizon and a past horizon and that they appear to themselves as temporal.,'[7]...

The stories of Sanu Lama, would agree with Merleau Ponty's claim that all consciousness is embedded in time; that perception is 'pregnant with its form' and that the unity in terms of continuity of time is provided by the passage of these perceptual experiences. But for Lama, what perceptual experience does provide me is a basis for my *comprehension* of existence in relation to me, while existence is what is presented to me. The former is an engagement. His stories draw an implicit distinction between the *fact* and my comprehension of the *fact as being* related to me. The former would constitute the objective meaning while the latter the existential meaning of time in relation to the present. The stories of Lama highlight that I *live* in the latter alone since the former brings along with it an inherent void since it essentially excludes me from its fold. This is perhaps why, if I am to make a record of *my* life (a kind of autobiography), it would not list the continuity of time in terms of the former but only in terms of the latter. It would list the comprehension of the then present and how it was related to me then and how the present is related to me now. Such a record would be a record of *my* historicity and not a linear record of the continuity of time itself. It would chart *my* history and not history per se. In the stories of Lama, the past and the future is not seen as the mere 'perceived perceptual experience' and the 'yet to be perceived perceptual experience' in the linear continuum with the perceptual experience of the now. Thus, the past and the future are seen as *my* past (the then present related with me) and *my* future (the way I would like to relate myself to future possible present), which form the horizon on the backdrop of which the present relates itself to me.[8] Thus in the stories of

Lama, the past and the present form epistemic backgrounds rather than ontological categories, that render the possibility of comprehending the present as meaningful in relation to me.

The past in the sense of an ontological category is seen as the present that is gone and the future as the present that is yet to come. But to view it thus is to impoverish it. On the other hand, if the past and the future are treated as epistemic categories, as in the stories of Lama, then the past can be seen as the horizon on the backdrop of which the present relates itself to me and is rendered existentially meaningful to me. Viewed thus the past and the future frames the present, enabling me to comprehend my meaning *in, and as a part of,* existence and thereby enabling me to engage in the present. The past and the future, as depicted in Lama's stories are characters in their own right and this is what makes a symbiotic relation between my past, my present and my future possible providing a sense of unity to my existence. Thus my present cannot be distinguished from my past and my future in terms of immediacy of their availability to my consciousness, or in terms of the degrees of their pellucidity and clarity. To do this would be to confuse the objective with the existential notion of time and the present with my present.

Lama's stories throw light upon the nature of the relation between my past and my future and the present. If the future and the past are the horizons in which I engage with the present to make it meaningful in relation to me rendering it as *my* present, then it is the present that makes possible the invocation of my past as well as my future—my past and my future exist only in so far as my present exists. All realizations, sweet or bitter, pleasing or painful occur only in the present. No Buddha can be born in the past or in the future. As the character from Lama's *Mṛgatṛṣṇa* understands that he must ensure that prince Siddhartha sees the *old man* and the *dead man* as he comes on his royal parade today if he is to meet the Buddha in the future, we too come to realize that even the hope for a Buddha in the future must take place in the present. Both *being* and *becoming* takes place in the present. Echoing a line of *Paroh,* we could say, 'All events take place in the present'. It is only through the present that the past and the future make sense. Lama highlights through his stories how my present has as its horizon only *my* past or *my* future. It is centered and rooted in the 'I' and the 'my', while perceptual experience of the presented present is not 'I' centered and abides by the principle of consensus in nature. When I 'perceive' this table having a hard surface beneath the surface where I have now placed my laptop, the underneath part of the table is immanently presented to me and not inferred, though my perception at the present is restricted to the surface of the table on which my laptop is placed. This awareness of the table having two surfaces is not 'I' centered but is rather provided to me in my very perception as the perceptual experience comes along with the horizon of the very being of the table. This is what lends objectivity to perceptual experience; lends objectivity to the present. But in case of *my* present, the 'I' plays a central role since *my* past and *my* future are exclusively mine and hence what the present *means to* me is 'I' centered as my present is situated only in the horizon of *my* past or *my* future. All that constitute my past and my future are in direct relation to the 'I'. That is to say that the 'I' is immanent in my past or my future and nullifies the void that the present brings along due to the absence of this 'I'. It is this horizon that the present is embedded in that ensures the relation of the present to me.

Thus, in the stories of Lama, time is depicted through the modalities of the past, present and future, where the trio is understood as those epistemic categories through which the entire existence unfolds its existential meaning to me, or the meaning of the present as it relates to me. Thus, for me as a 'being in the world', the only temporality is the temporality presented to me as *my temporality* in terms of my past, my present and my future, and existence is restricted to those "beings in the world' alone that relate to *me* through these modalities of time. Thus, in so far as the meaning of my existence is concerned, all that is central is the 'I' and the world related to it. It is not that the objective world in the linearity of time is 'real' and *my world* is an illusion. On the contrary, Lama's stories put forth the thesis that the only reality that 'I' comprehend is the one that is in relation to me and the world of objects presented to me but constitutes a mirages—a *mṛgatṛṣṇa*.

NOTES

1. I am indebted to Ms. Sandhya Pradhan who helped me in procuring the literary works of Sanu Lama all the way from Gangtok; to S. Lama for being kind enough to lend me his personal copies of those works that were unavailable elsewhere; to Ms. Rinzi Lama and Padmadhar Choudhary for helping me in reading the literary works; to Mr. Aditya Nain, Ms. Janavi Dhamankar, Ms. Suchi Vora, Mr. Yashor, and Prof. S.S. Deshpande and Dr. Medha Deshpande, for their valuable comments on the paper.

   The stories cited here are from a collection of his short stories compiled under *'Mṛgatṛṣṇa'*, R.K. Enterprises, Gangtok, 2006. (1st edition, 1990)
2. M. Merleau-Ponty, *The Primacy of Perception and Its Philosophical Consequences*, in 'The Primacy of perception and other essays on Phenomenological Psychology, the Philosophy of Art, History and Politics', ed. James M. Edie, North Western University Press, 1967, p.12.
3. To use Merleau-Ponty's terminology, perception does not merely provide me with sensory data upon which I impose a form and synthesize them to make them meaningful but that it presents itself to me *as* being *meaningful*. I do not, so to speak, infer the meaning of my perception as it presents itself to me by imposing a 'form' upon it. Following Merleau-Ponty, one could say that one does not involve oneself in an *'intellectual synthesis'* while comprehending the meaning of what is perceived. Merleau-Ponty writes:

   "...it is impossible, as has often been said to decompose a perception to make it into a collection of sensations, because in it the whole the prior to the parts ... the meaning which I ultimately discover is not of the conceptual order. If it were a concept, the question would be how I can recognize in sense data, and it would be necessary for me to interpose between the concept and the sense data certain intermediaries, and then other intermediaries between these intermediaries, and so on. It is necessary that meaning and signs, the form and matter of perception be related from the beginning and that as we say, the matter of perception is pregnant with its form."(p.50)
4. *Ibid.*, p. 12.
5. *Ibid.*, p. 13.
6. *Ibid.*, p. 14.
7. *Ibid.*, p. 21.
8. Given this understanding of time, we would be unable to formulate Zeno's paradoxes of motion as Zeno's motion takes place in linear time. For Zeno passage of time is always from one unit moment to another unit moment. It is perhaps for this reason that we do not encounter Zeno's paradoxes in the time that I *live* in.
9. *Ibid.*, p. 21.

13

Ki Jingsneng Tymmen and the Clan Elder

Esther Syiem

At their creative best, *Ki Jingsneng Tymmen* is a body of aphorisms that have been orally transmitted through the ages. They mark an important territory in Khasi thought for they capture the ambience of a culture with roots embedded deep in the oral practices of their ancestors, where the social and the metaphysical exist parallel to each other. The noted Khasi writer, Radhon Singh Berry, put them down in written form in a two volume work[1] first published in 1902, which will be repeatedly referred to in this paper. Although they are more than a century old, the aphorisms contained in two unedited volumes — are still used as literary text in schools and colleges for imparting Khasi culture to the present generation. Apparently repetitive to the modern reader, the very essence of orality lies in just this.

For purposes of the present study, this written rendition will be used as the primary, although not the exclusive, source. Within the scope of the discussion, the two volumes have been used as a means towards the larger end of understanding the structure of Khasi belief and value system. I will, however, have to go beyond them and draw from the oral sources that have fed the very foundations of Khasi society.

In this paper I will try to look at *Ki Jingsneng Tymmen* as a vital extension of the social, an outgrowth of the oral that has defined the Khasi way of life. It serves as a coalescence of Khasi thought. Many of the dos and don'ts found in *Ki Jingsneng*

Tymmen are still functional in modern life, the anchor that, ironically, seems to assuage but not alleviate much of the confusion in an increasingly complex society.

Ki Jingsneng Tymmen, reflect the vital chords of a society that has always believed in the existence of one supreme deity, *U Blei Nongbuh Nongthaw*, "God the Creator and God the Maker", and the life concurrent with such a belief; that the Khasi have come to this world only to *kamai ïa ka hok* or to "earn righteousness". The formulation of this body of sayings or proverbs and chants has been carefully shaped by a culture that has always preferred to explain its existence in mythic rather than in historic terms[2]. This is intimately connected with the elevation and installation of the oral to a position of centrality that was consequent upon the mythical loss of the written script[3]. The oral or the spoken word, *ka ktien*, rationalises the ultimate meaning of existence in a way that is geared towards the preservation of a mystical sense of life where the *rngiew* or the aura that radiates from an individual and even the entire community must be kept alive.[4] The individual or community may be measured in terms of the *rngiew* that gives it distinctiveness.

The *rngiew* is a numinous extension of personality, a lighted area that encircles an individual and spells out personality in several complex layers. Nourished by an inherent genius which is also the racial intelligence, it is an unselfconscious recognition of one's multiple strengths. This in itself produces positive waves that communicate themselves to others in multifarious and intangible ways. The *rngiew* speaks of an inner force that is difficult to conceal. In maturity it is almost tangible and is a natural protection against all negative influences. Even a child may possess a strong *rngiew* or be *eh rngiew* and, therefore, prove able to withstand the suppressive forces that may threaten him/her. Giving a child a name is the first step towards empowering its *rngiew*.

To be *jem rngiew* is to be opposite of *eh rngiew*; that is, to be abjectly prone to suppression or to be unable to contend with conflicting pressures of many kinds. In life one must make a conscious effort towards the development of a strong *rngiew*.

The *rngiew* is an integral part of personality in a way that is difficult to peel off. It is an organic accumulation of the experiences that determine the inner core and outer layer that constitutes personality. To put it simplistically, the person whose flag flies high at all times is the person whose *rngiew* remains uncontested, keeping marauders at bay.

At this point, an explicatory note is necessary to explain *Ka Niam Kur* or the "clan religion" originally practised by the Khasis. An emerging Khasi writer, Dondor Giri, has explained its origin and evolution in a recent article, *That Elusive Niam Kur (Clan Religion) of the Hynñiew Trep Geographical Landscape.*[5] Although it would not be possible to discuss this at length in this paper, the one indisputable fact that emerges is, the respect that the maternal uncle in the Khasi matrilineal society, evokes. Today, even in Christian families, he maintains an importance that is impossible to sideline. The appellation "orphan", for example, cannot be indiscriminately used, if the clan uncle and grandparents are still alive. This effectively points to the indispensable role that the clan uncle has to fulfill in respect of his clan. All belief remaining the same in the various clans or *kur*, "prayers, rituals, and sacrifices were usually performed by the eldest maternal uncle of the clan." His esteem within the clan and consequently within society, lies in his ability to negotiate the social and the spiritual, the physical and the metaphysical. He spells out the rationale for life by codifying existence for the clan and society at large.

As clan elder, Radhon Singh Berry perceives the value of the words that he transcribes, conscious that they will help in the maturing process of each individual *rngiew*. He must, therefore, take his role seriously in order to ultimately fortify the *rngiew* of the entire Khasi community. The motivating power of *Ki Jingsneng Tymmen* lies in the elder's consistent efforts to keep the symbolic Khasi flag flying high at all times, for the *rngiew* to be nourished and to grow.

Unlike the vast body of oral resources in African American Literature that evolved as stratagem to escape the white master, *Ki Jingsneng Tymmen* are straightforward, pithy reserves of philosophy and poetry, culture and literature. They come from a society that enjoyed the freedom of introspective and, especially, retrospective thought; the ancestors were unquestioned as the ideal repositories of wisdom and knowledge. They speak of the inevitable outgrowth of a society that has always placed great importance upon the spoken word, as it must continually harvest its own store of accumulated wisdom. This is both challenge and promise, for the spoken word has been perceived as a tool of immense potential, its full power understood only in maturity, hence it cannot be trifled with. Book One Section XXI warns against the dangers of negating the word.

The antecedents of the written version of *Ki Jingsneng Tymmen* date back to a period when the evangelisation of the Khasi and Jaiñtia Hills by the Welsh missionaries had gained momentum. As was inevitable in such cases, a number of Khasi intellectuals having benefited from a Western and in some cases a Bengali education, fought hard to preserve the unwritten in the written form. One significant result for the preservation of Khasi Literature and Culture was the compilation of *Ki Jingsneng Tymmen.*[6]

I have dwelt at length on the Invocation as this forms a significant prelude towards the understanding of the Khasi belief and value system. The rest of the *jingsneng* grow from the Argument that must be placed before "God and man". These *jingsneng* harvest the racial wisdom of the Khasis which is communicated through chants or *ki phawar*, an inbuilt means of public communication. As a genre they form a vast store of undocumented knowledge. To some they come as naturally as speech itself. They use subterfuges such as humour and exaggeration to express themselves.[7] In *Ki Jingsneng Tymmen, ki phawar* are an inevitable outgrowth of a natural skill with words, wielded for the benefit of its audience. They display a sense of poetic propriety in their ability to combine the oral techniques of poetry with moral injunction.

The Invocation is a request for empowerment from God. Three epithets have been used to describe Him: *U Blei U Trai U Kynrad U Bastad*, God the Maker' the Master the All-Knowing One. Although this is a formulaic beginning for all occasions, it is always at the altar of *U Blei* that the elder, the priest or the medicine-man invokes empowerment for the performance of their respective roles within their respective arena. The four lines of the Invocation sum up the Khasi world view, God above and supplicating humankind below. By virtue of his maturity, his position of responsibility and his contribution to society, the elder takes on the mantle of a higher responsibility to impart to a younger generation the values that must be nurtured for safeguarding a God-centred life.

When *Ki Jingsneng Tymmen* were first published, it may be inferred that Radhon Singh Berry, was the ideal image of the Khasi elder, representative of a particular breed of Khasi men who have a manifest responsibility towards God and the younger generation. One must also see him within the perspective of the written version, as the poetic persona responsible for the projection of culture and religion. Upon him too, rests the ability to wield the spoken word with sharpness and insight. He is retracing a path that has been traversed several times over in the past by similar men of responsibility. The one significant difference lies in the fact that the path is now a *written one.*

The verses resonate with the accumulated voices from the past, repeating the essence of *Ka Akor Khasi* or the Khasi code of ethics. He emulates the spoken word through an oratorical display of language and maintains the formality reserved for occasions such as these, when the entire *kur* or clan gathers around the elder to be taught in its ways. Consequently, one must understand that the identity of the persona, of Radhon Singh Berry the author, is not as important as the ritual moulding of Khasi identity through the spoken word. This has been the compulsion of a society that perceives continuity primarily in its ability to teach, impart to and instill in its younger ones, the spoken word.

Hence the emphasis upon truth, *ka hok,* in the second line of the Invocation as a way of life ordained by God, is also a metaphoric self-anointment by truth that elevates the elder to the position of seer. The second line envisions a generation that is made perfectible by its inner sighting of truth, equipping itself to lead the younger lot. The third line roots the race upon an important dimension, the clan, paternal relatives and the family: *kur, kha* and *ïing*. These have been crystallised and are reflected in everyday conversation in terms of *Kamai ïa ka hok*, to earn righteousness, *tipbriew-tipblei*, to know man and to know God, and *tip-kur tip-kha*, to know one's maternal and paternal relations.[8]

In as much the same way as caste is an all-pervasive entity in Hindu society,[9] so is the clan to the Khasi way of life. These three corner stones of existence for the Khasi finds analogy in the three hearth-stones that make up the Khasi hearth –*ki mawbyrsiew*. These special stones that ring the fire, represent the strength and unity of a family and hence, of society. The glowing fire in the kitchen has been a cultural symbol of abundance and continuity, especially when a household can still boast of the presence of a member/members of the older generation who, in the literal sense keep its embers alive, by warming themselves around it. Ideally it is around the hearth, not in the shade of a tree, that character is formed and values forged, where the spoken word reigns supreme and wisdom conferred to the eldest. Thus *sawdong ka lyngwiar dpei*, around the hearth, is an actual configuration of the oral-based foundations of the Khasi way of life.

The last line of the Invocation completes the circle of life. Where the third line is suffused with considerations of the present, family and society, the next line makes a vertical move back to God. Having fulfilled one's duty to family and society, one anticipates further guidance from above so that the respect of "hearth and home," "clan and society" may be kept intact. The elder also pleads before God not to bring humiliation upon the race. The Invocation is a sensitive indicator of the priorities of a community, made clear in the written version of *Ki Jingsneng Tymmen*, through its elder, who is both the medium through which values are being processed and constantly refined and the prime actor in this public arena.

It must be emphasised that in Khasi society, gender roles are never ambiguous.[10] The spokesperson for the clan and society, in most instances, can never be a woman. In Khasi matrilineal society at present, much debate has been generated over the equality of the sexes. Gender inequality is evident in all spheres, where many men and women, knowing that they have to move beyond their designated roles, are yet unable to disentangle themselves from the time warp that they are trapped in. However, this is a paper that looks at Khasi society in its ideal state as it flourished in a fairly insular setup.

Thus the elder is usually the eldest clan uncle. He makes it his business to be the moral watch-dog of the clan and of society. Among Khasis, male prestige has always been synonymous with the man's decision-making abilities, his capacity to shape and change society. A man who is *ksan rympei rem dorbar* becomes the object of ridicule. The phrase refers to a man who argues and debates only within the realm of the domestic, literally in front of the hearth, normally associated with women and children. At public meetings or durbars, however, in front of equals, he remains mute. As a consequence, his *rngiew* as a *rangbah* or a man is seriously challenged. Men have been identified with the public realm of policy-making whilst women have been identified with the private realm of the domestic, looked upon as custodians of society. According to oral sources, one of the reasons why men surrendered lineage to women was for safeguarding the clan-name in that age when men constantly went to war. Hence it was for pragmatic, rather than essential, reasons that women were given custody of the clan-name.[11]

Ki Jingsneng Tymmen are steeped in the lore of a matrilineal society that gained strength from its oral deliberations. The word *sneng* in the third line of the Invocation, focuses upon the oral ability or the actual reaching out through the spoken word to one's relations, to advise, warn, teach, bring to consciousness; a responsibility that did not sit easy on the shoulders of many men. The compulsion to *sneng*, therefore, became the prerogative of a few who had the aptitude for keeping the channels of communication open, firstly with God and then with his fellow human beings. The emphasis even in the written version lies in this ability to shape character and reality using the spoken word.

The spoken word becomes a tool of great power and cannot in any way be trivialised. As inextricable as *Ki Jingsneng Tymmen* are from the oral so are they doubly dependent upon the oral discourse that must shape society in its continual evolution. There has, however, been a noticeable break in this discourse. In the wake of British colonisation and the development of the Khasi alphabet by Welsh missionaries the compulsion to forge newer horizons of thought and refine character has never regained its original impetus. In her book[12], the historian Helen Giri, has discussed this impeded evolution at great length. Though not a conclusive factor, the very fact that *Ki Jingsneng Tymmen* have never been updated or revised says everything about the erosion of the oral and the failure of the written to replace it at this level of Khasi thought.

In his own way, however, Radhon Singh Berry has tried to stay the loss by crossing over to the written, thereby preserving whatever oral wisdom was accessible to him at that critical moment in Khasi thought. He is strongly grounded in the lore of Khasi life because he, like all his predecessors, experiences closeness to God and to people. This is a qualifying virtue that empowers him as it has others before him, with a strong sense of mission, to establish the two-way communication, both vertical and horizontal, that will enable him to interpret and clarify values in society. He closes the Invocation by reminding everyone, that once he takes on the mantle of elder in order to *sneng* others, God will, henceforward preserve society from itself and keep disgrace away–an apt preamble to a discourse that has always remained God-centred. One must keep in mind that the elder is not addressing himself to the reader but to a listening audience in which Radhon Singh Berry, the author subsumes personal identity for a public and mythic role.

The opening line of the first verse calls up all the nieces and nephews, the clan at large, children and grandchildren, *ko pyrsa ko ïing bad ko khun ko ksiew*, to pay heed to the words of advice to come. This roll call follows a precise order in a society that is *kur* or clan oriented. A sure sense of tradition is then evoked in the words that lead up to the next line where both boys and girls, *"shynrang, kynthei, ngan sneng eh rngiew"* are expected to pay close attention to what is being imparted. In trying to understand *Ki Jingsneng Tymmen*, one must pause awhile to take in the ambience of a social situation in which nieces and nephews have taken predominance over one's own children.[13]

The twin roles of the man, as clan uncle and as father to his children, follow this particular order. He fulfills both roles judiciously but sometimes with significantly more emphasis upon the former. There is a recognisable sense of continuity when plenty of nieces and nephews, children and grandchildren gather around the clan elder to listen to his words, ensuring by their youthful presence the growth of the clan as a whole· A balance is created whereby every clan uncle fulfills his duty to the clan; whilst the man as father has a supportive role to play in the clan of his wife and children.[14]

The elder begins by cautioning the young against the ills of bad manners and a lazy lifestyle. Reprehensible habits are explicitly denounced, examples of which, form the bulk of many verses. The poetry arises out of illustrations that re-construct life in a chanting usage of idioms, *ktien kynnoh*[15], that spills over into language thick with hyperbole, imagery and metaphor. The first book is lined with analogies taken from nature illustrating the fall-out of bad habits and an indolent mind-set. Thus children are warned never to snatch things away "like a monkey", never to give or take anything "facing back" to someone, a taboo, much like the antics of a fleshless phantom from the underworld whose intentions are ambiguous. One is cautioned against recklessness towards nature and the elements, *ka ding ka um, ka dieng ka maw*, for this would definitely bring about accidents and ugly injuries of all kinds.

The path to be taken must be the middle one of moderation. In Section VII of Book One, a litany of rhyming couplets marks the route to be taken in one's daily life. The justification for such a life lies in the elder's insistence that everything roots back to God Himself. The last couplet hones the litany back to a lifestyle that is based upon calculation and deliberation, *da mut da khan, wat sarong, wat kyreit,* free of arrogance, for this mars clarity of thought. These are fundamental to an existence that is oral-based.

A visible legacy of these moral precepts may be seen in the way guests are treated even today. *Kwai, tympew* or betel nut and leaf, must be offered after sometime; picking up a broom to sweep the room while they are still present is an insult, explicit in its message. And if one were to pass in front of them in order to leave the room or walk through to another room, one would have to walk bent from the waist down as a mark of respect and apology for entering upon the other's private space. Rules for hospitality are laid down in Section XII of Book One where specific instructions, for example, are given about the ways of serving extra lime when giving betel nut to others –not on the tip of a knife for this would seem like a ritual performed for the sacrifice of animals; an insult to others but on a betel leaf, the right way up.

Sections XXIX and XXX of Book One and Section XXII of Book Two, deal with marriage, an important milestone that must never be crossed impetuously. Family background and equality of social status are significant criteria as are the importance of informing both father and uncle. Nothing specific is said about marriages having to be arranged by them[16]. As love marriages have never been an exception in Khasi society, it is imperative that each individual must take care that the friendship they entertain, which may lead to a permanent relationship, is not a tabooed one, that is, exogamous.

Section XXX lays down six important guidelines for a responsible life, some of which are: never to enter into relationship that is taboo, never to lie as this will shorten one's life, the repercussions of embezzling money, the offensiveness of adultery that may even lead to death. The list continues in other sections too, but the bottom line is that these excesses are taboo not only on earth, but in the eyes of God: *Baroh hynriew kim dei tang ha pyrthei / Sang bad pap ki long haduh khmat U Blei.*

The *Jingsneng* of the clan uncle are uncompromising and explicit. But before any further discussion and for purposes of clarification, the difference between the two concepts, that of *ka pop*[17] which is synonymous with *ka lait ka let* and *ka ryngkang ka palat* (mistakes of omission and commission); and *pap ka sang*, (incest and taboo) must be made[18]. As stated earlier, the clan is a pervasive entity that determines even the severity of sin. *Ka pop* is not as heinous as *ka pap ka sang*. *Ka pop* or *ka lait ka let* and *ka ryngkang ka palat* are human mistakes that are pardonable since they do not challenge the authority of the clan. Even if they do, they do not necessarily undermine it.

These may be petty instances of crime and in extreme cases, even murder[19]; but as long as motives are sufficiently understood as not impinging on the *sanctity* of the clan, they can always be justified "in the eyes of man and in the eyes of God". The oral aspect has an irreplaceable role to play at all occasions. Cleansing rituals and supplications may be appropriately offered at such times and, the reasons for such occurrences deliberated upon and closely weighed and examined in order to purge the cycle of any curse that may follow.

In *ka pap ka sang,* however, when the authority and sanctity of the clan is acutely jeopardised, the culprit / culprits must meet with dire consequences. Preservation of the clan in its sanctity has been the abiding concern of Khasi society. The individual has identity and significance only in respect to his / her position in the clan. Therefore a person's actions, good or bad, will always impact the family and the (maternal) clan to which the family belongs. Thus when taboo is committed, the entire clan meets to deliberate upon it. Taboos such as the murder of an uncle by a nephew or vice versa, intra-clan marriage, incest, demands immediate redressal because these violate the sanctity of the clan.

Actions such as these usually result in de-recognition and expulsion from the clan. Meanwhile the information must be made public. The culprits have to set up a different life elsewhere, but their past will dog them as inevitable questions about their clans will always come up in their adopted place of domicile. In rare cases, the death sentence is pronounced and the entire clan engages in the communal killing. The act of killing is looked upon as a necessary evil in the interests of clan sanctity. The ritual process of purification requires intense effort and great oral skills on the part of the clan elders in order that the clan be cleansed of the stigma of the taboo and of any boomerang effects thereof[20].

There are nuances buried in *Ki Jingsneng Tymmen* that may be understood only by a Khasi. In the course of my discussion I have attempted to tease out some of them. The *jingsneng* are layered with meanings that speak of a lifestyle with a highly evolved oral culture that has thrived for hundreds of years. Book Two begins by explicating upon a social hierarchy based upon seniority. It exhorts all youngsters to take heed of the wisdom and instruction imparted by their elders. The clan elder is once again reinstated in his proper place for the discourse to continue. Verses leading up to section VII weigh the priceless value of the spoken word: *ap dngong ïa ka ktien ba kren ki rangbah,* literally to wait patiently for the word to sound from the elder.

This leads to a further discussion on the verbalisation of words: never to trivialise words by using them aimlessly, by name-calling, or when addressing others, to always use their full names in order not to mar their *rngiew*. Should one's name be heard in the distance, one must always wait for a second and a third call, for in the first instance, it might only be the beguiling call of a ghoulish spirit. Odd numbers spell trouble and people going about must walk in even-numbered pairs[21] to deter bad luck and harm. Section X spells out the ways by which people are to be greeted and *kwai, ïympew* to be shared in a spirit of friendship. Section XI elevates the priest and medicines man to a position of respect not to be taken over by anyone else least of all, one's parents. He is described as the arch debater, the necessary link to God who will speak on behalf of all humankind.

In Book Two the elder continues his discourse, discussing serious issues related to life and death, sickness and sorrow, and the responsibilities, amongst others, that are related to marriage, clan and God. In Sections XLI to XLIV women are cautioned against excesses of behaviour, they are portrayed to be the intellectual inferiors of men and, all the similes used to illustrate them, describe them as "custodians", *Ka lukhimai/*[22] *Ka nongri ïing, nonglum khih lum kamai.* In following a path replete with dangers of all kinds, there is warning against allowing a woman to lead the way. In leading the way himself, the man symbolically obstructs danger and the enemy is deterred from attacking, knowing that the woman will "cry aloud for help", *Man ka kam u shynrang uba haphrang, / Man ka kam ka kynthei kaba ïap ang*. Men have always been perceived to be protectors and guardians. Men are also warned against a life of irresponsibility for it brings its own nemesis, examples of which abound in plenty.

A sense of retributive justice is inbuilt in Khasi thought. This is reflected in its mistrust of people with deformities, Book Two Section IX, for the belief is that, these are retributions for indiscretions of word or action. Consequently too, the razor-edge path that the elder has to traverse, lies in choosing the right words and setting up the appropriate arguments "before man and God" so that they do not backfire or prove to be ineffectual[23]. The combinations and permutations that the argument takes, has the ability to convict, condemn, cleanse or purge. The Khasi believes that it is humankind's (*u khun bynriew*), prerogative, at the altar of God, to "argue and define", "disclaim and reclaim", to "erect" words of supplication or defense. The phrase *ïeng rangbah u briew, Ap jutang U Blei,* depicts the archetype of the clan elder who literally "stands before God as man" (as opposed to a child), knowing that God waits for him "to speak so that the word be fulfilled". The clan elder combines the dual role of priest and prophet, *u kñi uba sait uba pynkhuid* and *u kñi uba sneng uba kraw*. In his capacity as priest he "expatiates and cleanses", "purges and propitiates"; and as prophet, he "warns and denounces", and is the "mouthpiece of God".

Hence the oratory that forms the backbone of *Ki Jingsneng Tymmen*, stems from an intrinsic ability to communicate through the chants or *ki phawar* in a public setting. One must remember that only a few have the inbuilt ability to wield them. These are, therefore, special in terms of the "chain of authority by which {they} are remembered".[24] After the introductory dedication, where links are established and the pattern set, they navigate a metrical rhythm that occupies, especially in an earlier oral set-up, a mental space replete with the aesthetics of the moral and repeatedly expressed for a specific ethical purpose. They draw their inspiration from nature itself as they unravel the path to be trodden. These *phawar* negotiate time and space, faith and values and are entrenched within the racial psyche, from which they have always been culled out by the dedicated few. The written version of *Ki Jingsneng Tymmen* documents this constant process of re-defining and re-processing thought at a particular stage in the development of life in the Khasi and Jaiñtia Hills.

Almost as a premonition of changes to come, the Epilogue to Book One questions the fate of the Khasi code of ethics. And the question that arises as a consequence of reading these *phawar* is, that if oral deliberations have become defunct, in a society that is pushing forward to meet the challenges of the day, as there has been no updating of these *jingsneng*. How does one reclaim one's oral roots? Would it be in terms of the past or in the digitised terms of the global village? Questions relating to the future of Khasi morals are fired off by the elder in the Epilogue to Book One, but since he continues with the second volume, one deduces that he is forging ahead with the kind of zeal that comes only with the dedication of a bard or a seer who refuses to submit to alternative value systems. The foresight and dedication of the clan elder must always remain unimpeachable.

NOTES

1. U Radhon Singh Berry, *Ki Jingsneng Tymmen shaphang Ka Akor Khasi ha ka rukom Rwai Phawar Part 1 and Part 11*, rpt. Shillong: Ri Khasi Press 1959.

2. This refers to the commonly held belief that the Khasis, even today, refer to themselves as a group of the seven families who descended from heaven to settle on earth. The other nine stayed on in heaven.

3. According to oral sources the man chosen to receive the script from God, was caught in a flood. Unlike his counterpart from the plains, the *dkhar* who kept his within the safety of his knotted pony tail, the khasi, put his in his mouth. In the event of crossing the river, he swallowed the script, thus depriving his people of a written script.

4. Refer to Dondor Giri Nongkhlaw's article on "That Elusive *Niam Kur* (Clan Religion) of the Hynñiewtrep Landscape", *Indian Theological Journal* Vol No 1 Jan –June 2007.

5. Dondor Giri "That Elusive Niam Kur (Clan Religion) of the *Hynñiewtrep* Landscape."

6. Refer to Bijoya Sawian Dey's introduction in her translation of *Ki Jingsneng Tymmen.*

7. The article by Juanita War in *Lest We Forget,* Shillong: Seven Huts Enterprise 1994 explains the *khasi phawar* in simple terms.

8. R.T. Rymbai writes about this in his article, "Some Aspects of the Religion of the Khasi- Pnar in *Khasi Heritage,*" Shillong: Ri Khasi Press 1979.

9. Sudhir Kakar and Katharina Kakar in *The Penguin Yearbook* 2008 p. 138.

10. This is an aspect that is important to Khasi society, that men and women have assigned roles. Many oral sources bear witness to this.

11. It is a commonly known fact that men were the original keepers of the clan name. Ref. also to Donbok T. Laloo's documented tale in *Ki Paju lyngkot,* Shillong: Don Bosco Press 1970.

12 *The Khasis under British Rule,* 1824-1947, New Delhi: Regency Publications 1998.

13&14. Refer to *Tribal Institutions of Meghalaya,* ed. By S.K. Chattopadhyay, Guwahati: Spectrum Publications, 1985.

15. A way of speaking unique to the Khasi.

16. Arranged marriages are rare in Khasi society.

17. *Pop* is a loan word and probably came at a later time.

18. This differentiation has not been made in Bijoya Sawian Dey's translated version.

19. The clan still rules supreme in many families and instances of killing by the clan is, though rare nowadays, still a probability.

20. This is the *tyrut* or the curse, that continues to have a superstitious hold on society.

21. This according to oral sources, was what happened to the inhabitants who were eaten up by the *thlen* or the serpent when they went marketing together in odd numbers.

22. *Lukhimai* is the spirit associated with wealth. Women are supposed to be of single strength whereas a man's strength consists of twelve layers. Another oral saying warns against such time when women would begin to "crow like a cock", for it spells subversion of all kinds.

23. Diviners and priests have to be cautious in the way that they put up their arguments so that nothing backfires and no consequent destruction wrought.

24. Hugh Miles in his book *Al Jazeera: How Arab TV News Challenged the World* (London: Abacus 2005) speaks about how the spoken word holds sway over the written and the importance attached to it in the Arab world. This is no different from many communities in the east. Amongst the Khasis, wedding invitation cards have no real credibility. It is the personal call at home that solicits response from invitees.

14

Generating Knowledge: Khasi-Jaintia Oral Texts

Soumen Sen

The Centre of Advanced Study (CAS) in the Department of Comparative Literature expects us to explore issues related to Literature as Knowledge System and suggests studies of texts in terms of "a complex of knowledge systems that include practical concerns of everyday living along with larger world-views unique to the culture." For exploration of these issues and studying texts in terms of a complex of knowledge systems, the cultures of North-East India can offer an extremely apt illustration.

In this kind of project, especially when the focus is on the north-eastern region of India, two kinds of dilemma may crop up. The first one involves the definition of 'knowledge'. The answer is perhaps simple if we take a positivist position. Viewed from this position, knowledge is, no more and no less than 'scientific knowledge', based on observable phenomena. The emphasis is on 'factual' evidence, a belief in 'objective' method, and the production of 'verifiable' results. Opposed to this position, the post-modernists would say: "Science once taken to be the touchstone of legitimate knowledge has lost its assumed unity" (Lyon.1994 (2002):16). They would further say that it is important to realize the growth of knowledge as a social and cultural process as well. The process of such delegitimisation begins with this realization. The traditional sense of 'knowledge' thus decomposes.

Why then do we call it a dilemma? The concept note from Jadavpur CAS says: "We propose to formulate a new vision for the study of literature focussing on its entity as a cognitive system that has its own dynamics of knowing and making known". But what is 'knowing' and 'making known' and what is 'cognitive system'? Is cognition a synonym for knowledge that designates ideas and discoveries as processing of informations? In such processing the starting point is the World or to be precise, Nature. Confronted with the complexities of nature, man attempts its appropriation. This is 'Knowledge' acquired by empirical observation. It is 'Knowing' and then 'making known'. Is literature a vehicle for such acquired knowledge or does it create knowledge itself? What then is the type and nature of that knowledge? Can knowledge be prescribed through literature and made not only 'known', but also to 'observe'? Is there any 'prescriptive' reality beyond 'reality?'

In such a situation, a set of constructs appears that a society gives to itself, to grapple with the problems of survival and everyday living. The intent is simple and two issues are critical – prominence of information and communication and facilitation of social cohesion and relationships. Norms are designed and passed on as 'tradition'. Should we call them a set of livelihood strategies, which are inextricably integrated with socio-political, and religions institutions, social and kinship networks and belief systems? If we take them as "knowledge systems" (and we ask why not?) then the time-honoured ways of thinking about knowledge evaporates. Knowledge then appears as a discourse and its structure reflects the structure of the society, which produces it and whose needs it satisfies. It is not as simple as "knowing", the knowing of external observable phenomena and making it known, but prescribed to be known and absorbed in everyday living. Such forms of discourse generate a kind of social authority to ensure social wellbeing and spawn all the sectors of knowledge system called folklore. This approach however does not negate altogether the claim of science. The empirical observation of natural phenomena and the world around in order to use the multiple resources given by nature is used to the advantage of the people and the society. Since rational knowledge is obtained from experiences, both "natural" and "social", its categories are only the results of an intellectual process considered useful for the felt needs of the society. Ultimately, folklore stands for the process which, even etymologically means the lore (wisdom, knowledge) of a group of people (folk).

This identity of folklore was ignored for a long time, even by the folklorists. It was once identified as verbal art or oral literary expressions only. Though with a change in attitude and attention to field work in recent years, the other sectors—customs, art, craft, architecture and performances—received weightage in folklore studies, they were taken more as artistic expressions than as sources and generators of knowledge. Traditional research based on customs and systems and worldview is a recent phenomenon and that too in a limited scale. Earlier customs and habits were taken as the survival of the past, even of a primitive stage. Folk beliefs, according to the survivalists, are the inherited magical and mythical notions crystallized into customs. They were not considered as knowledge. Even when attention was paid to 'cognition' which was filtered through all the senses, its implications were not taken as all-pervasive as the current notion of folklore would demand. Cognition is used as a synonym for knowledge that designates thought as processing of information based on empirical observations and experiences.

This is the major and the second dilemma that we encounter while treating oral literature. An initiative has recently been taken by the UNESCO for defining folklore and traditional knowledge as if they are two distinct and separate identities. Folklore is taken as traditional artistic expressions of a community and traditional knowledge is viewed as the carrier of information, inventions and discoveries. This approach is reflected in recent attempts to protect 'Intellectual Property Rights' based on a debate encouraged under the auspices of the UNESCO. Realising that the conventional intellectual property laws do not adequately cover or protect expressions called folklore, national governments were advised to enact their own laws. In India a draft for a bill has been prepared with a title "Folklore and Traditional Knowledge (Protection and

Regulation) Act 2006", and significantly folklore and traditional knowledge have been defined separately. Folklore is defined as "production consisting of characteristic elements of the traditional artistic heritage developed and maintained by a community reflecting traditional artistic expectations of such a community." Notable are the words 'artistic heritage' and 'traditional artistic expectations', circumscribing the sphere of folklore. Though traditional knowledge in the draft refers to tradition-based literary and artistic works like designs, symbols, masks and performances, the emphasis is on scientific discoveries, undisclosed information, inventions and intellectual activity in the industrial and scientific fields. Forgotten completely, perhaps unconsciously, is the fact that folklores and oral texts both are tools for knowledge. Obsessed with the conventional concepts of and distinctions between 'art' and 'science' we perhaps still go by the view that 'oral tradition' is 'verbal art' or literary creations such as myths and tales that reflect 'fantastic and fanciful realities', while 'knowledge' is synonymous with dissemination of information and techniques obtained through intellectual enquiries, discoveries and inventions.

That folklore, with both its literary and artistic expressions and scientific observations, discoveries, inventions and practices, is knowledge has to be recognised. This knowledge is equally 'obtained' and 'generated'; the obtained sector is 'livelihood essentials', while the other is 'livelihood strategies'. One is obtained and taught; the other is designed and communicated. Literary and artistic expressions are the modes of communication.

With this perspective, I refer to North-East India, rather one of its part, the Khasi- Jaintia Hills of Meghalaya. Here we see the bulk of 'literary expressions' as oral due to the predominance of the so-called 'tribal' population, most of whom were non-literate till the middle of the 19th century and their language was non-scripted. Although they can boast of written literary texts that emerged during the last seven or eight decades, they still live in the glory of oral tradition.[1]

Oral literature occupies the major part of their literary

history [2]. If we are to look for an indigenous knowledge system, our only source will be folklore, including oral literature. The other sectors (of folklore) are customs, performances and material arts including crafts, architecture and technology. The last can be designated as 'science' based on enquiries and inventions, whereas the first three are essentially cognitive creations and discourses, involving strategies with words, metaphors and symbols as mental categories to prescribe realities. Words are chosen, symbols created, structures designed, in order to understand reality and its requirement and to translate it into an appropriate worldview.

Khasi-Jaintia

The Khasi-Jaintias belong to the state of Meghalaya, in the north-eastern region of India. Two of the five major groups who were earlier known in the outside world by the generic term Khasi, come from the same stock. Although the migration routes cannot be firmly established, scholars have traced a relationship between the Khasis, the Mons of Mayanmar, and the Khemrs of Kampuchia. A linguistic and cultural connection has also been sought between them and Austric groups such as the Ho–Mundas of central India. The Khasi-Jaintias, hence, are identified as a Paleo-Mongoloid group, with Mongoloid physical attributes, speaking a language of the Mon-Khmer branch of the Austric family. With a number of dialects, the standard language now is known as Khasi. They are designated as "scheduled tribe" under Indian constitutional arrangement.

Social organization focuses on the institution of matrilineality. Descent is matrilineal, and residence is matrilocal. The mother controls household property and religious rites. She is succeeded by her youngest daughter. However, the eldest son enjoys authority in making decisions in *durbariing* (the family council) even after shifting his residence to his wife's mother's household after marriage, and play a dominant role in the *durbarkur* (Clan-council).

The matrilineal principle is also evident in the clan-centred religion, which revolves around a triad: *Ka Iawbei* (the progenitress), *U Thawlang* (the progenitor) and *U Suidnia* (the eldest son of the progenitress*)*. A basic tenet stresses the consciousness of kinship principles. Thus religion is essentially a shared experience with predominantly female principles being ritually propitiated. Female deities relate to general welfare, production of wealth, and protection from diseases and other calamities, while male deities' duties include defence of state, village territories and markets.

The folklore of Khasi-Jaintia has largely been an expression of the clan, ethnic and religious identities and of the sanctity of the matrilineal order, social organization and political system. It undoubtedly corresponds to acquired experiences but its distinctiveness lies in a preference for prescriptive communication with a demand for conformity to initiate an individual into a communal life and renewing and strengthening shared convictions. In the process it surely appears as a strategic knowledge system.

Oral Texts: Narratives

Of all the narratives, the most fanciful is the one we usually designate as myth. The folklorists' usual perception of this category of narrative is not much different from the meaning offered by any standard dictionary which describes it as purely fictitious usually involving supernatural persons, actions or events and embodying some popular idea concerning natural or historical phenomena (*The Oxford Universal Dictionary*). When William Bascoon, in the fifties of the last century, categorised oral prose narratives as myths, legends and tales, he followed the prevailing concept of myth set in the supernatural world with divine and semi-divine heroes as principal protagonists. In Homer's time they were either superhuman (and divine) or men 'favoured by gods'. Not that this approach to myth is wholly untenable. It is set in the creative mode in which man confronts mythically his society's belief system in an amythic (should we say indetermined) and eschatological epoch and is essentially the verbal part of religious ritual.[3]

But, can we look at "myth" in a different way that current exercise in folklorography[4]' demands? This genre of oral narratives, with its ritual connection, is, in most cases, taken as explanation of religious thoughts and practices. The human being is, by nature, a *homo religiosus,* and is assumed to be bound by religious canon in which he or she has been indoctrinated.[5] In many cases, this indoctrination happens through mythic narratives. The religious connection of myth thus becomes obvious. But it is equally true, and in most cases, that it is used to 'indoctrinate' the people in clan and kinship norms and socio-administrative system. The narrative establishes its social authority acting from a 'mythological' space. It carries a mytho-symbolic message for clan-solidarity and ethnic identity. The reality the myth describes is prescriptive asking the people to adhere to and observe. Its annual enactment in a ritual event and festival reinforces a command raised to a belief in the system.

This is exactly what happens in the case of a "myth" and its ritual-festive enactment in Khasi-Jaintia Hills. Both the narrative and its enactment are ideology sensitive, rooted in the social system and belief. Attitude toward the belief content is the essence of the genre and its enactment. Since the belief is the stimulator and the purpose of the narrative and its enactment and it being the 'instigator of the legend dialectic' (Degh,1996:33), then why can the narrative once classified as "mythical", not be called a legend? To put it precisely, the people (in our study the Khasi-Jaintias) believe in the narrative's authenticity in describing their ancestry and identity, the religious and ethnic juxtaposed. Such belief often makes a mythical narrative, a legend[6]. I will suggest further that, such legends stimulates knowledge as historical and social and everyday livelihood strategy.

The Khasi-Jaintia narrative of *Ki Hynniew Trep* (the seven huts), conventionally called 'Origin Myth", is an example of such strategy. It is repeatedly referred to, to enhance identity consciousness. The people prefer, even today, to call themselves 'the children of Ki Hynniew Trep', "in times of storm and stress, of stir and strife, whenever there is a call for the unity" (Rymbai, 1998:166). The cultural (and religious as well) symbol of this narrative is consistently used in identity assertion. In this perspective, and following Linda Degh's prescription, it can very well be called a Belief Legend.[7]

The strategies involved are manifold. Firstly, to establish a common ancestry of the Khasis and the Jaintias,the two sub-types of a common stock, secondly, to uphold clan solidarity and kinship norms through a theological construct of three tenets or commandments. This also justifies the triad formed of three ancestors to be remembered and propitiated in ritual events. Thirdly, they reiterate the matrilineal kinship principles and fourthly, juxtapose religious and ethnic identities. Later, this principle was reiterated in a nationalistic movement with a declaration that "a Khasi is a Khasi when he adheres to his religion *Ka Niam Khasi*".[8] Finally the narrative intends to establish the authority of both an administrative system and a Leader, given a semi-divine status, enjoying both secular and religious authority.

The *Ki Hynniew Trep* narrative has a number of versions. In one account, God initially created sixteen families who stayed with him in heaven and commuted between heaven and earth by means of a ladder in the shape of a tree on a hilltop known as *sohpetbneng*. Later, seven of these families known as *Ki Hynniew Trep* expressed their desire to remain on earth. God granted their wish and removed the ladder.[9] In another version, in the golden age after creation, man had a personal relationship with God and commuted between heaven and earth. But, in the course of time, *Ki Hynniew Trep* drifted away from God to choose their own ways and thus the golden ladder(the tree of *sohpetbneng*) collapsed. Later they repented and god forgave them. The story of man's repentance and God's forgiveness goes like this: A huge tree enveloped the earth in darkness (signifying Man's spiritual crisis) with its overspreading branches and leaves and was ultimately felled by God.[10]

In yet another version, of *Ki Hynniew Trep*, God gave them three commandments, projecting the essence of *Ka Niam Khasi*, the Khasi religion. These are *Kamai Ia Ka Hok* (Earn Righteousness), *Tip Brieed Tip Blei* (Know Man and Know God) and *Tip Kur- Tip Kha* (Know maternal and paternal kinship). These commandments were received through the leader (*Syiem*) U Lakriak whom God had chosen as his representative on earth.[11]

All the versions of the narrative constituted the expression of deeply-felt emotions and compulsions important for survival. The most essential part of these is the knowledge intended and generated to ensure ethnic identity (the concept of *Ki Hynniew Trep*) and clean solidarity (*Tip Kur-Tip Kha*, one commandment of *Ka Niam Khasi*, the religion). The indoctrination happens at the level of belief and the acceptence of the narrative as 'true'. Significantly, the religion, *Ka Niam Khasi*, attaches importance to a triad, *Ka Iawbir* (The Mother- ancestress of the *Kur*, the maternal kin group), *U Thawlang* (The Father- the ancestor of the paternal kin group *Kha*), and *U Suidnia*, the maternal uncle (the eldest son of *Ka Iawbei*), who also represent different kinds of authority in the organisational setup of family and clan councils extended to a sort of 'early state' known as *Hima*, with a leader (*Syiem*).

The *syiem* is chosen on the principle of matrilineal succession. Theological ideology is closely linked with social arrangements from family to ethnic level via clan and kin systems. *Ka Niam Khasi* is an example of putting divinity to mundane levels of existence. The authority of the leader (*syiem*) is established when he is declared as God's representative on earth, and through him the people receive the commandments of religion, which in turn, are close to social regulations.

Knowledge of social concern as livelihood is generated in the same fashion in almost all the *genres* of oral narratives. Some prescribe norms, some explain taboos such as incest taboos, some prefer aetiological takes, with juxtaposition of 'religion' and 'science', combining livelihood essentials or realities and strategies for decent living with commitments to social codes. These explain the interplay of the forces of nature, mankind's relationship with the ecological order and animal world, and other such lofty topics, the stories generating knowledge to encourage conformity with kinship norms, socio-political customs, and religious–moral codes. Hence a major *genre* in the Khasi-Jaintia narrative repertoire is the fable, which is simple and straightforward in structure. Fairy tales are more limited in number.

It is possible to read a good number of tales to substantiate the statement. But, I will use, for the sake of being brief, one or two representative narratives, conspicuous in their attempts to communicate clear-cut messages.

An approach, accepted in the community as a type which in the typology is called parable[12], but can also be taken as aetiological, takes care of a socially prohibitive norm, which at the same time attempts to explain natural events like the sunset and sunrise. The story is simple without much structural complication:

> A day was fixed for a dance festival, and all living creatures turned up in their grand costumes. They danced throughout the day until, when they were tired and were about to depart, there arrived the Sun and the Moon, a sister and brother, and they too danced. Everyone jeered at them, saying that it was evil that a brother and a sister should dance together. In shame, the Sun went off and hid herself inside a cave, called *Ka Krem Lamet Ka Krem Latang*. With her withdrawal to the cave, the earth was enveloped in darkness. Man had to find out ways and means to induce the Sun to come out again. Finally, a cock was used as a messenger and, with its crowing, the Sun reappeared. There was light again.[13]

Besides 'making known' a fact of nature and the association of the cock's early morning crowing with sunrise, the story also includes a social norm. In the matrilineal Khasi-Jaintia society, marriage within the class is strictly prohibited and any such relationship is ordained as incest. Members of a class are brothers and sisters. Society faces a spiritual as well as structural crisis in the event of a violation of the prescribed practices. Punishments are prescribed for any such violation.

Incidentally, couple dances are not encouraged in Khasi-Jaintia Hills. In most of the festivals boys and girls dance separately as in the case of the ritual of *Ka Pomblang* popularly known as Nongkrem festival held annually at a place called Nongkrem, and dancing couples are frowned upon. In one festival only, *Laho*, girls and boys take part, but with "permission from God" through the authority of the *Syiem*, the leader. There is a story:

> When *Syiem U Laxriah*, the leader of the seven huts (*Ki Hynniord Trop*) came to his people with messages from God, all were happy. They felt that the occasion be celebrated with a festival of dance. *U Laxriah* resorted to a type of divination to decide on the manner in which the dance was to be performed. It was decided that if the froth came to the brim when a gourd-pitcher was filled with rice-beer, it would be taken as God's approval. If otherwise, it would be taken as His disapproval. *U Laxriah* first asked for permission for a dance in pairs – a male and female. Froth did not come up and so it was taken as God's disapproval. Then *U Laxriah* sought the permission for a dance by three or two boys and a girl in the middle, froth came up to the brim signifying God's approval.[14]

Other such stories can be picked up to demonstrate that folktales are not simply the reflection of reality ('mirror of social environmental life' as almost an adage in stereotype research), or used to explain (making known of the known), to entertain, to educate and inspire, but also are designed to convey a message, to communicate the essentials of existence. The message is usually straightforward, not allowing much room for multiple interpretations. The strategies used in the construction of these texts are determined by components involving manipulation of codes – moral, social and political – for the purpose of attaining socio-political gains and to ensure cohesion and stability. There can never be any doubt about the directness of these strategies, and, perhaps, there is no scope for chosen interpretations. The communication that is intended in such narratives is deliberate and prescriptive even if clothed in linguistic codes such as metaphors. Such codes, although used for artistic effect, never neglect culturally relevant requirements. As I have discovered above, even the marvellous called 'myth' is often designed keeping in view these requirements.[15]

A good number of narratives tell history – history of social and political formations. The narrative of *Ki Hyanniew Trep* is the forerunner among them. This, along with some other legendary stories, like the story of *Ka Pah Syntirn* which explains how the *Hima* (a pre-state political formation) of Shillong came into existence and that of *Ka Lih Dakha* explaining establishment of a Kingdom, known as Jaintia kingdom, as an extension of a *hima*, Hima Sutnga, have been very carefully designed. There are a few more such narratives and the designs are strategic to explain socio-historical compulsions for adjustment in social and administrative structures and the growth of some hegemonic order and social stratification. We cannot tell for certain but can assume from the straightforwardness of narration that these strategies evolved when the society had undergone significant transformation through rearrangement in landholding and agrarian relations abandoning the egalitarian structures. A few clans, the original settlers in the area, were allowed to enjoy a privileged position with private rights on land and holding oligarchic states and authority in the council of the Hima (*Durbar Hima*) with a positive say in the choice of the *Syiem*. They had even been declared (or was it that they occupied their domain in a special way to declare themselves) as aristocrats (*bakhraw*).[16]

Other Texts

So far I have discussed, in much detail, how the Khasi-Jaintia oral narratives were constructed to convey socio-politically relevant messages. In the process there also evolved a 'knowledge system'. Some non-narrative texts also appear as parts of this system.

Take for instance the proverb, which is said to be a short pithy saying in common use to express some truth ascertained by experience or observation. It is said to arise as part of everyday discourse and as expressions of popular collective experience. Current researches, however, have raised a few questions about this approach to proverb studies. The analogical form of the proverb establishes it as evidence of a point of view. But the question is: whose point of view and whose viewpoint is intended to be legitimised? Questions have been raised whether they sometimes demonstrate a covert agenda to ensure a hegemonic system [17] In many a cases proverb takes the shape of aphorism to advise a course of action, legitimising it as part of wisdom. Such wisdom is not an acquired wisdom but a prescriptive one although there are proverbs which carry wisdom acquired through experience and observation like weather proverbs and proverbs explaining human nature when the aim is to comment on social relationship and an attitude is expressed or prescriptions are made to treat one section of people vis-à-vis others, the proverb loses its claim of being expression of collective experience. It then appears, to the mass or the community as sayings of the ancients based on their experience and wisdom and needs to be believed and followed as past for present and future actions.

In Khasi-Jaintia society there is great respect for 'tradition' which includes the sayings of the ancients. The distinction between proverb and aphorism is often blurred. Most of 'the sayings' that appear as proverbs in the usual categorization are believed to be sacrosanct as they are parts of 'tradition'. They are also taken as ancient tenets to be respected and followed.

To be brief, I will talk of a few such tenets that have a bearing on the role and status of women. My reason for picking up these tenets is the reflection of a sort of contradiction. The Khasi-Jaintia society is matrilineal. By the simple logic of the system, women in this society enjoy a status different from women in most other traditional societies. The prejudices that are noticed elsewhere are relatively absent here. One tenet, *Long Jaid Na Ka Kynthei* (From the woman springs the kin), assigns women respectful status as mothers in the matrilineal order as keeper of the domestic group (*Ka nongri iing*). Significantly this is contradicted by some others denying them any role, decision-making role in particular, in both domestic and socio-political domains. The brother of the mother, or her eldest son is the decision-making authority at the domestic level in the family council (*durbar iing*). The women are also debarred from joining village council (*durbar shong*) and the council of *hima* (*durbar hima*). In upholding such systems, tenets were created, such as, *Adur lanot, wei ba la Kynih ka'iar Kynthei* (Woe the day when the hen begins to crow), or *Ka akor khasi ka khang bah kynih ka iar kynthei ne said thma ha durbar*, which forbids women from wearing masculine attire and speaking before the *durbar*. Their status were fixed as that for a *Lakshmi*, the Hindu goddess, as the keepers of the domestic group with an assigned role of looking after the wellbeing of the family but they lose their honour if they crow like a cock (*Ka nyerthei Ka long Kum Ka lykhimai*). Such aphorisms keep women 'in their place'.

Advices are offered, norms are communicated in almost all the *genres* of folklores. The Khasi-Jaintias have an ethno-specific genre, called *phawar*, a distinctive form of oral poetry with a musical quality between chant and song. It consists of a rhyming couplet, which may be sung or chanted to pipe, stringed instruments or percussion on occasions ranging from rituals to sports competitions. Different categories of *phawar* reflect these different performance situations; at socio-religious occasions such as births, marriages, and funerals; at celebrations of military victories or of successful hunts; during archery competitions (regarded as national sport); at the erection of megaliths to commemorate the ancestors); and during festivals. Whatever the occasion, the *phawar* carries a socially relevant moral message. Each line of the couplet is usually divided into two parts. Both parts of the first line are sung by a "rhyme setter" with a chorus taking up the second line presenting the couplet's message – for example, *U Hyndeh ka jalyngkhan, U sohbrap ho ia ka skei / Wat (eit leh kam by mman, io timpap ka blei* (He pants for curry leaf, for the passion fruit, ho! For the deer. / Never do what is evil, or the goddess will curse).[18] A few such messages can be listed:

> Do not put too much trust on your own self-will. It is ungrateful.
> Such unbriddled freedom (wilfulness) has no regard for taboos.
> It transgresses limits set by the ancients.
> Be wise, live according to the rules.
> Stand on truth in death and life.
> Oh children, do not give in to self-will and unbridled freedom. Only then will you be able to please your ancestors, the family triad.[19]

These, and the messages communicated in the narratives and their texts, are taken as traditional wisdom given by the ancients. Hence they are to be honoured, and are honoured. But, were they not generated with strategies involved in manipulation of codes in order to effect control? These do constitute " a complex of knowledge systems that include practical concerns of everyday living along with larger world-views unique to the culture".[20]

NOTES

1. For a more detailed discussion, see Sen, 1988, 1992, later included in Sen 2004.
2. For the history of Khasi Literature, see Bareh, 1979 and Sten 1990.
3. For further study of such concepts of myth, see Jason 1975: 37-41.
4. I use the term 'folklorography' consciously to distinguish it from the usual terms like folklore research or folklore studies as is done in the case of historiography much in use in current trends in history-writing. In such an approach history is viewed as catastrophic and always in crisis. It therefore challenges any sort of 'master code' (Frederic Jameson. See Brooker, 2003:124), explodes " bland continuity" (Walter Benjamin. See ibid), and presents history as a constellation contradicting the conventions in writing history. The Indian (Bangla as well) equivalent of historiography is *Itihascharcha*. I am inclined to use *Lokosamskriticharcha* or folklorography opting for an open-ended approach, capable of gazing at the phenomenon called folklore and challenging all sorts of conventional typification and definitions. I allow a researcher to discover reality in multiple levels.
5. See Degh, 1996:35.
6. *Ibid.*
7. *Ibid.*
8. See, Rymbai 1979 and Sen 1989.
9. Rymbai 1979:110.
10. See, Mawrie, 1981:5-6.
11. See, Sen 1985 :168-69.
12. See, Mawrie, *op. cit.*
13. *Ibid.*
14. See, Sen 1998.

15. I have discussed in how these requirements were kept in view in designing socio-politically relevant texts. See Sen, 2001.
16. How it happened is a long story. To read that story, see Sen 1985 and 2004.
17. To know about these enquiries about proverb, see among other, Yankah, 1991; Basgoz, 1993; Sen 1997.
18. See, Simon, 1978.
19. I am grateful to Prof Juanita War of North Eastern Hill University, for these examples and their translation.
20. The Concept Note, CAS, Dept of Comparative Literature, Jadavpur University.

REFERENCES

Bareh, Hamlet 1979. *A Short History of Khasi Literature*. Shillong : Don Bosco.

Bazgoz, Ilhan. 1993. "Proverb Image, Proverb Message, and Social Change." *Journal of Folklore Research* 30: 2/3.

Brooker, Peter 2003. *A Glossary of Cultural Theory*. London: Arnold.

Degh, Linda 1996. "What is A Belief Legend?" *Folklore*: 107.

Lyon, David 1994. *Post Modernity*. Buekinghan: Open University Press.

Rymbai, R. T. 1979. "Some Aspects of the Religion of the Khasi– Pnar" in Hipshon Roy (ed) *Khasi Heritage*. Shillong.

Seng Khasi. 1993. "Christian Missions and the Indagenous Religion of the Khasi–Pnar" in. Soumen Sen. (ed). *Religion in North-east India*. New Delhi : Uppal.

Sen, Soumen 1985. *Social and State Formation in Khasi – Jaintia Hills: A Story of Folklore*. New Delhi : B. R. Publishing.

1989. "The Changing face of Khasi Religion" in James A. Beckford and Thomas Luckmana (eds.) *The Changing Face of Religion*. London: Sage.

1992. "Literature and Paracentral Literature: The Khasi Paradigm". In Amiya Dev (ed). *Papers in Comparative Literature Calcutta*. DSA, Comparative Literature, Jadavpur University.

1997. "The Proverb: A Hegemonic Discourse? *Dialogue: The Journal of North – East India Forum for English Studies* II.

1998. "Folk Narrative and Social Reality in Matrilineal Khasi Society" in Jawaharlal Handoo (ed). *Folklore in Modern India.* Mysore: CIIL.

2001. "For King's Sake : Narratives as Designer Texts". *Indian Folklore Research Journal.* 1.1. 2004.

2004. *Khasi-Jaintia Folklore: Context, Discourse, and History.* Chennai: National Folklore Support Centre.

Simon, I.M.1978. "A Note on Khasi and Its Development as a Literary Language" in J.N. Chowdhury. *The Khasi Canvas.* Shillong : Chapala.

Stem, H.W. 1990. *Khasi Poetry: Origin and Development,* New Delhi: Mittal.

Our Contributors

Mrinal Miri taught Philosophy in St. Stephen's College, New Delhi and in North-Eastern Hill University. Chancellor of Rajiv Gandhi University, Arunachal Pradesh, he was also Director of the Indian Institute of Advanced Studies, Chairman of the Indian Council of Philosophical Research and a member of the National Advisory Council of Government of India. He received the Padma Bhusan for his contribution in the field of education and literature. He is also known for his very significant contribution to the understanding of issues related to tribal culture. Among his major works are *Identity and the Moral Life* (2002), *Tribal India: Continuity and Change* (ed., 1993) and *Philosophy of Psychoanalysis (1997).*

Sujata Miri was Professor of Philosophy and Dean, School of Humanities, Education and Languages, North Eastern Hill University, Shillong. Her publications include a series of books on tribal cultures of North-East India as well as a book on paintings on themes from the North East. She is also a novelist. She is at present engaged in directing a research project committed to the understanding of the worldviews of the Aos of Nagaland and the Garos of Meghalaya.

Sukalpa Bhattacharjee is Associate Professor of English in North Eastern Hill University. She has authored *Postcolonial Literatures: Essays on Gender, Theory and Genres* (2004) and has co-edited *Human Rights and Insurgency: The North-East India* (2002) and *Ethnonarratives: Identity and Experience in North East India* (2006). She has published extensively on Critical Theory, Gender Studies and Multi-Ethnic Literatures of the United States.

L. Joychandra Singh started his career as a lecturer in Government Colleges. He later became Secretary, Manipur State Kala Academy and Director of Jawaharlal Nehru

Manipur Dance Academy. He has a book entitled *Chinungi Sana Loktagi Paibiraklo* and has translated from English into Manipuri.

Meghali Goswami teaches in the Department of Fine Arts, Assam University, Silchar and is an Art Critic. She also specialises in Art History and New Media Art and has published extensively in national and international journals. Her book *Motifs in Mughal Architecture: A Critical Overview* is in press. Meghali is also the editor of *Canvas*.

Rimli Bhattacharya is currently teaching in the English Department, University of Delhi. She has been the Rama Watumull Distinguished Indian Scholar at the University of Hawai'i at Manoa and ICCR Visiting Chair at the Department of South Asian Studies, University of Pennsylvania. She has published extensively in the area of performance, visual history and social contexts of Bengali theatre. Her current interest is also in the area of primary education and she has been involved in various national and international collaborative projects. Rimli is also a distinguished translator. Her volume entitled *Songs in many Tongues: Lullabies and Play Songs in Ahomiya, Mizo and Kumaon* is forthcoming.

Epsita Halder teaches Comparative Literature at Jadavpur University. She works in interdisciplinary areas of narratology, cultural studies and performance studies. She has several publications in the area of performance studies and is currently working on Karbala narrative traditions of Bengal. Epsita is also a creative writer.

Debashree Dattaray is Assistant Professor at the Department of Comparative Literature, Jadavpur University. She was Visiting Scholar on a Fulbright Doctoral and Professional Research Fellowship at the State University of New York. Her areas of interest are Comparative Indian Literature, Canadian Studies, Oral Traditions and Gender Studies and she has several publications in her field.

Margaret Ch Zama is Professor, Department of English, Mizoram University, Aizawl. She specialises in Tribal Literature and Writings from Northeast India. She has written extensively on tales from Mizoram, on the future of folklore, on globalization and tribes of India and various related issues. Her book entitled *Northeast India: The Insider's Definition* is in press.

Prasenjit Biswas taught philosophy at ISM, Dhanbad, IIT Mumbai and Guwahati and Assam University, Silchar. Currently he is an Associate Professor of Philosophy at NEHU, Shillong. His major works are *Ethnic Life-Worlds in India's Northeast (Co-authored with Chanaan Suklabaidya,* 2008) and *The Postmodern Controversy: Understanding Richard Rorty, Jacques Derrida and Jurgen Habermas* (2005). He has co-edited a volume with C. Joshua Thomas entitled *Construction of Evil: Myths, Narratives and Discourses from India's Northeast* that is forthcoming. He also writes regularly for *The Statesman,* New Delhi on contemporary politics in India's Northeast.

Pravesh G. Jung is presently a faculty of Philosophy at the Department of Humanities and Social Sciences, IIT-Bombay, Mumbai. His works are usually in the area of Wittgensteinian philosophy, General Semantics and Peripheral Philosophy and he has made important contributions in the area.

Esther Syiem teaches English Literature at North Eastern Hill University. She is a bilingual poet and has two volumes of poems, *Oral Scriptings* and *Of Follies and Frailties of Wit and Wisdom* and a Khasi play *Ker Nam.* She has written extensively on Khasi folk literature and has a forthcoming book entitled *The Oral Discourse in Khasi Folk-narrative.* Esther is also the author of *The Idiom of the Allegorical Mode: A Study of Six Novels.*

Soumen Sen is former Head of the Centre for Literary and Cultural Studies, NEHU and the Director of its Programme of Folklore Research and Archive. Some of his most important publications are *Folklore: Identity and Development in the Context of North-East India* (2010), *Folklore, Tradition and Urbanity* (2010) and *Khasi-Jaintia Folklore: Context, Discourse and History* (2004). He has several edited volumes to his credit and has also published extensively in Bengali. He is a member of several professional bodies, both national and international.

Index

Abo-Tani,124
Adorno,46
Ahom kings, 41
Akas,14
Atiya Guru Sidaba, 32, 33
Angami, 122, 138, 139
anthropological, 1, 51, 79, 125-26, 133, 144
anthropologist, 133
anthropology, 79, 125-26, 140
Ao, 122,138
Apatani, 122,132,133,134,141
Arambam, 58, 62, 85
architecture, 42, 175
art, 1- 2, 8 - 9, 12, 19, 38, 40
artist, 38
Arunachal Pradesh, 14, 67
Assam, 20, 21, 41- 44, 50, 63
author, 9
authorship, 9

Badal Sircar, 85
Basil Gray, 41
Barnes L Mawrie, 130
Benjamin, 46
Bhutan, 48
Buddha, 154
Burma,50
Cachar,50
China, 48, 67
Chittagong,50
Chola-Cholum,77
Christian, 50, 135
Christianity, 65, 69
Churra, 116-18
cognition, 175
cognitive, 13,38,46, 114
communication, 28
community, 22-23, 25-28
craftsmen, 10
creation, 13
culture, 8, 11, 13, 39, 46, 49, 51
cultural, 1, 23, 37, 48, 50, 62
culturally, 1, 3

diachrony, 129
Dondor Giri, 159

Earth-God, 14
East Asia, 59
elephant, 41, 42-43
empathy, 7-8
epistemological, 5, 94-96, 98, 108, 133
epistemologies, 1, 13
epistemology, 4, 5, 27, 104, 127
ethnic, 2, 53, 68
ethnically, 1
ethnicity, 48, 50-52, 64
ethnophilosophical, 128-29
ethnophilosophy, 121

fiction, 9, 20
folk art, 9
folk dance, 9, 10
folk literature, 9
folk lore, 51, 93, 97, 175-76, 178, 186
folk narrative, 1
folk song, 11
fuoion of horizon, 11

Hastividyarnava, 38-39,40,42-43,46
Heidegger, 6, 9, 19
Hornbill Festival, 65-67

imitation, 9

Imphal, 35, 84
indigenous, 13, 93

James E Young, 20
J H Hutton, 138

Ka Akor Khasi, 161
Ka Iewma, 15
ka ktien, 158
Kanglei Haroba, 33
Kanhailal, 77, 85, 88
Kant, 19
K G Subramaniyam, 62
Khezakhenoma, 123
Ki Jingsneng Tymmen, 157-59, 160-65, 168-69, 170
K N Pannikar, 81
Kohrian, 9
Kuki,78

Lai Haraoba, 32-47, 53
legend, 14, 15, 178
life-world, 1-2,38-39
Lushai Hills, 50

Maiba,35
Maibi,35
maikei ngakpa, 32
Mamang Dai, 123
Manipur, 32-33, 35, 50, 54, 57, 61, 66-67,88-89, 123
Manipuri, 36-37, 53, 55-59 60-61, 63, 64, 72, 86-87
Maori, 93
Meitei, 32,34, 57, 78, 81, 86
Merleau Ponty, 149, 152
modernity, 4,6, 45
Moirang Haraoba, 33
Mughal,41-44
Myanmar, 48, 65

Naga, 50,65-66,69,76;86,93
Nagaland, 65, 70, 106

otherness, 93 ,143

Paul de Man, 27
Peddo-Dodum 13
Penakhongba,35
performance, 41, 58-59, 87, 97, 102, 175
performative, 36, 79
phenomenology, 28
philosophy, 1,2, 19, 32
pictorial narration, 39
playwright, 62

Rabindranath Tagore, 40, 63, 89
Radhon Singh Berry, 157-59, 161, 164
rasa, 77, 90
Rasa-lila, 78, 87, 89
Ratan Thiyam, 76, 77, 80, 82, 84-85, 89
Rengma,123
rngiew, 158-59, 168

Sekhar Das, 24, 26, 28-29
Sitking-Kedding,13
South East Asia, 59-60
Stephanie Ross, 38
story telling, 2, 21, 96,106
Sumi,123
Surma Barak Valley, 20-21
Sylhet, 17,20,50

Tanghkul Naga, 50
Temsula Ao, 97
Thangjam Manorama, 88
Thang-Ta, 76-77
theatre, 36, 55, 68, 80, 82
Theodor Adorno, 46
Tripura, 50, 59-60

Umang Lais, 33
unbounding, 48, 50, 51

Wari-Leeba, 83-84, 90
William Bascoom, 178

□□□